THINGS EVERY GUITAR PLAYER SHOULD KNOW

Fretboard Basics, Strumming Styles, Iconic Gear, Powerful Chords, Legendary Guitarists, and So Much More!

DALE HICKS

ISBN: 978-1-962496-20-9

For questions, please reach out to
Support@OakHarborPress.com

Please consider leaving a review!

Just visit: OakHarborPress.com/Reviews

FREE BONUS

SCAN ME!

GET OUR NEXT BOOK FOR FREE!

Scan or go to:

OakHarborPress.com/Free

TABLE OF CONTENTS

INTRODUCTION

Did you know that over 50 million people in the United States have played the guitar, making it one of the most popular instruments? Globally, more than 10 percent of the world's population—or roughly 700 million people—play or have played the guitar at some point in their lives. The guitar industry is worth $10 billion, and it only continues to grow. More people want to learn guitar every day.

If you're wondering why the guitar is so popular, the answer is simple: It's one of the most versatile instruments, with a foothold in every genre and musical style. Not only can you play whatever you want on the guitar, but you can also take it with you. All you need is a simple carrying case or strap over your shoulder and you're ready to spread your music to the world.

If you're interested in learning how the guitar could be the perfect form of creative expression for you, then you're in the right place! Playing guitar can improve memory, coordination, and even your mental health.

The guitar traces its roots back 5,000 years to the ancient civilization of Mesopotamia. It has continued to evolve into the instrument you're familiar with today.

By the end of this book, you'll be ready to jump on the stage and have a greater appreciation of the wonder that is the guitar. You'll also learn how the guitar has changed and influenced cultures worldwide. But it's always a good idea to begin with the basics— and the best place to start is with the instrument itself.

CHAPTER ONE:
THE GUITAR

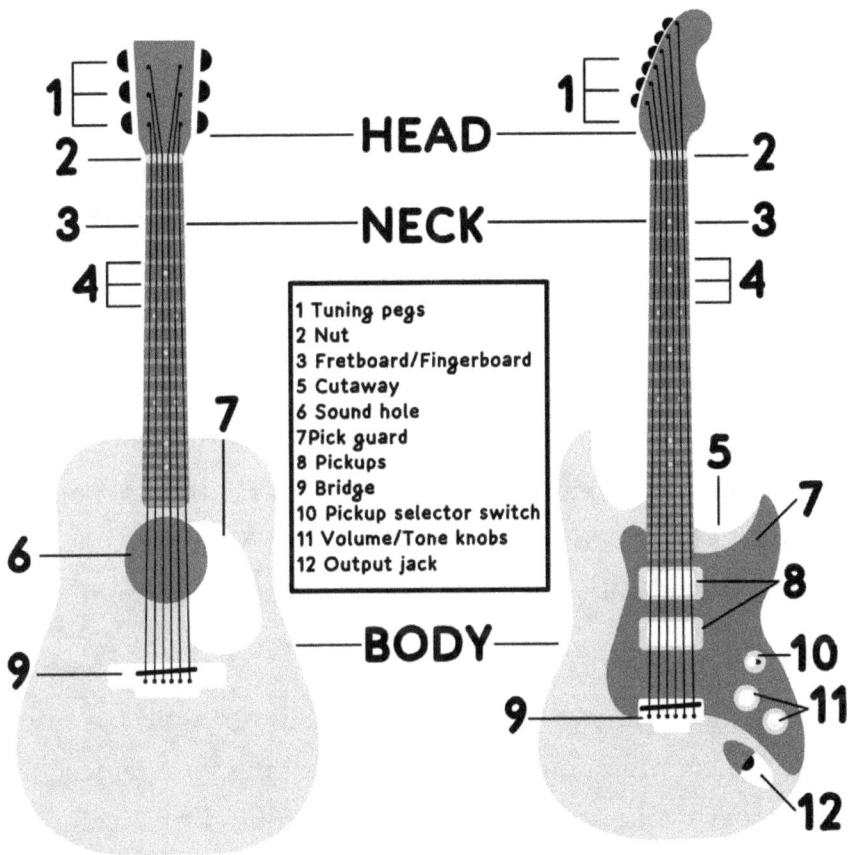

1 Tuning pegs
2 Nut
3 Fretboard/Fingerboard
5 Cutaway
6 Sound hole
7 Pick guard
8 Pickups
9 Bridge
10 Pickup selector switch
11 Volume/Tone knobs
12 Output jack

HEAD

NECK

BODY

BENEFITS OF
PLAYING GUITAR

Playing the guitar activates both the right and left hemispheres of your brain. The analytical left side controls the rhythm and technical aspects of guitar playing, while the creative right side is in charge of melodies and emotional expression.

As you play guitar, these hemispheres work together through the corpus callosum, a bundle of nerves that connects the two sides of your brain. Some studies from Harvard have shown that playing an instrument actually increases the size of your corpus callosum, leading to what's commonly known as "musical intuition."

Many studies have been performed on music and the effect it has on the human body. This research suggests that playing an instrument like the guitar can lead to higher IQ scores due to the increased connectivity between the two sides of your brain.

When you play your guitar, you'll also improve several other skills without realizing it. You'll hone your fine motor skills because of the precise coordination needed to create music. Playing guitar also improves your auditory processing abilities by activating the auditory cortex. This increased sensitivity allows musicians to better understand and recognize emotions in other people's voices. Additionally, reading music develops your visual processing skills.

Another possible benefit of playing the guitar is improving your cardiovascular health. Slow, soothing guitar music often calms anxiety, which can reduce your blood pressure. Music activates your parasympathetic nervous system and helps your body reach a state of relaxation.

As your blood pressure lowers, so does your heart rate. Your muscles also relax. Without tense muscles, you'll experience physical relief, and combining this with deep breathing often leads to better overall health.

While the physical benefits of playing guitar might seem obvious, it provides emotional and mental benefits as well. Making music is an effective way to process emotions, providing a way to release frustration, express sadness, and celebrate joy. Having a constructive outlet for your feelings goes a long way toward emotional control and health.

Even if reflecting on your emotions isn't your goal, playing music can also offer a diversion from the stress and worry of everyday life. When you're fully immersed in music, day-to-day concerns fall away and leave you with a new experience to focus on. You can reduce stress by playing music for just 30 minutes each day. Down-tempo music can even reduce stress by 61 percent—much like yoga or meditation.

Just playing your guitar triggers your body to release feel-good hormones such as serotonin, dopamine, and endorphins, which all have a calming effect. Music can also reduce levels of the stress hormone cortisol, causing you to feel better and more relaxed as you play.

Guitar can also improve your communication skills; after all, music is the universal language! In fact, studies have proven that musicians' brain waves tend to synchronize when they play together.

The long-term benefits of playing music are well documented. Musicians are 64 percent less likely to develop dementia as they get older because of the increased brain activity that comes with regular practice. Just as crosswords and other mental exercises can help avoid cognitive decline, so can reading music, memorizing chords, and developing the coordination to create music.

Before you can reap these benefits, you'll need to take the first step of buying or renting a guitar. While both acoustic and electric guitars are good to play, guitarists tend to develop a personal preference. Both styles have key differences, advantages, and drawbacks.

HOW AN ACOUSTIC GUITAR WORKS

An acoustic guitar creates music by transforming the energy from string vibrations into audible sound. Plucking a string creates vibrations, and the speed of vibration determines what sound the instrument produces. Thick strings create lower pitches, while thin strings create higher pitches.

These vibrations travel down the strings to the bridge, which then transmits them to the body of the guitar. The wooden body acts like a speaker, projecting the sound your strings create. Just like an empty cave, sound echoes in the hollow body of your guitar to amplify the music.

Next, these magnified vibrations escape the body of your guitar through the sound hole. Finally, they travel as sound waves to reach your audience, allowing listeners to enjoy the music you've created.

THE ANATOMY OF AN ACOUSTIC GUITAR

Learning the basics of guitar is the first step to mastering this remarkable instrument. Once you understand how the different parts of your guitar work together to create music, you'll be one step closer to mastering it.

HEADSTOCK

The top part of the guitar where the strings are connected is called the *headstock*.

TUNING PEGS

Tuning pegs, also known as "machine heads," are located where the strings connect to the top of your guitar. These cylindrical knobs allow you to tighten or loosen the strings to adjust their pitch. The string posts keep the strings secured, and "worm" gears maintain tension to keep your guitar in tune.

Obviously, it's important to tune your strings properly. Otherwise, the sound your guitar makes won't match the notes you're trying to play.

NUT

This small white piece contains cut-in grooves to hold the guitar's strings in place. Generally made of plastic, bone, or graphite, the nut maintains an appropriate distance between strings. In other words, it prevents problems such as buzzing and poor intonation.

Bone is considered by many to produce a higher-quality sound than cheaper materials like plastic. However, each material produces a unique sound, and some guitarists have a different preference.

Along with keeping the strings evenly placed, the nut also controls the distance between the strings and the fretboard, which is commonly referred to as *action*. If the nut is set too high, it can cause finger pain and fatigue. On the other hand, if the action is too low, you may experience rattling.

NECK

The neck is the long, thin part of the guitar that connects the headstock and body of the guitar. The frets are located on the neck, and this is where you put your fingers to change the pitch of each string.

FRETBOARD

This thin surface holds the frets in place, providing a surface for the strings to be pressed to create different notes.

FRETS

These thin strips on the fretboard divide the neck into different sections. Each represents a different pitch, or *semitone*, of an octave. When you press the strings, the resulting note is determined by which fret you use.

POSITION MARKERS

Inlaid position markers on the fretboard serve to provide visual guidance when you're playing. The most common position markers are circles, but some guitars have custom-shaped inlays. These marks are traditionally placed on the third, fifth, seventh, ninth, twelfth, and fifteenth frets. The twelfth fret generally has a unique position marker to make it easier to find.

TRUSS ROD

Usually made of steel, the truss rod provides stability to the guitar neck to prevent it from curving from the tension of the strings or atmospheric changes. If the neck becomes deformed, the action of your strings will be affected.

NECK JOINT

The neck joint connects the neck of the guitar to the body and comes in three varieties: set-neck, bolt-on, and set-through.

A set-neck joint—the standard for acoustic guitars—typically uses a dovetail joint and glue to attach the neck and body, which are manufactured separately. The sturdy connection makes for a warm, full sound as the energy from the strings flows freely through the instrument. The resulting resonance is perfect for creating the traditional sound and feel of an acoustic guitar.

Bolt-on neck joints don't use glue; instead, they're formed with screws and a metal plate. The slight gap that bolt-on joints leave between the neck and body produces a brighter, snappier sound than the set-neck. While set-necks are much longer lasting, bolt-on joints are the easiest and cheapest to manufacture. They're also the most straightforward to repair and replace.

The third type of neck joint is a through-neck, where the guitar's neck and body are formed from one piece of wood. This joint produces the longest sustain and smoothest tone but is only made by a select few manufacturers. While it's also the strongest joint, once it breaks, it's impossible to repair. Therefore, only the highest-end guitars are made with the through-neck.

STRINGS

Most guitars have six strings of various thicknesses, with one being the thinnest and six being the thickest. Stringed instruments date as far back as 1500 BCE, and string technology has steadily improved over time. The oldest strings were made from readily available materials like animal intestines, gut, hair, or plant fibers.

It wasn't until the Renaissance that the string was reimagined and gut strings were wrapped in metal to create a new, deeper sound. Into the eighteenth and nineteenth centuries, gut strings were still the most popular. However, other materials were gaining popularity, including silk cord wrapped in metal.

Once the Industrial Revolution hit, the mass production of steel led to steel strings. By the mid-nineteenth century, most guitar strings were made of steel, which created a bright tone and higher volume that worked well for folk and blues musicians who played to large crowds.

In modern times, strings can be made of several different materials, including nylon, fluorocarbon, and synthetic materials. Thinner materials are usually made of a single material, while thicker ones are wrapped with nylon or metal.

BODY

The body is the main part of the guitar where the notes from the strings are amplified and sustained.

SOUNDBOARD

Also known as the "top," a guitar's soundboard amplifies the strings' sound and is the true soul of the guitar. The quality and construction of your soundboard will determine the quality of your guitar.

Soundboards are made of lighter wood, which transmits sound better than heavier materials. Interestingly, different types of wood handle sound differently. For instance, cedar produces warmer tones than spruce, which is more punchy and versatile.

Along with solid wood tops, some guitars also have laminate wood that's similar to plywood but very thin. This type of material is affordable but doesn't vibrate as much as solid wood, leaving the sound somewhat flat. Laminate wood tops can be more durable and easier to maintain since they aren't as affected by outside sources as wood. However, they don't improve over time the way solid wood tops do.

If you're new and looking for a starter guitar, a guitar with a laminate wood top is a budget-friendly option. Once you become more proficient, you may consider upgrading to one with solid wood.

While it might be tempting to customize your guitar by adding stickers or other decorations, this may affect the sound quality. Guitars are designed specifically to ensure the best sound possible, so it's best to avoid muddying up the sounds.

SOUND HOLE

The round hole in the middle of the soundboard is called the *sound hole*. It provides room for the soundboard to vibrate, then amplifies the music. This opening allows pressure to escape and boosts the volume.

Sound holes are traditionally round, but less common shapes are available as well, including D-shaped, triangular, and elliptical holes.

ROSETTE

Although adding your own decorations to a guitar isn't recommended, some guitars come with built-in embellishments such as wood inlays. One common example is the rosette—a decorative inlay around the sound hole.

Rosettes aren't just for looks; they also help to prevent cracks that may form around the sound hole from spreading across the soundboard. This makes the guitar both more visually unique and structurally stronger.

BRIDGE

The bridge anchors the guitar's strings to the body while giving them enough freedom to vibrate. Bridges are made from a range of materials, including wood, metal, plastic, and even bone.

A saddle on the bridge supports the strings, holds them in place, and transmits their vibrations into the body through small pegs called *bridge pins*.

BRACING

Hidden within the guitar body are bracings that provide structural support to the soundboard. These wooden supports, or *struts*, are glued to the soundboard to prevent string tension from deforming the top. While several structural variations are used, we'll focus on the two most common forms: x-bracing and fan bracing.

X-bracing uses two braces, which cross to form an *X* near the middle of the guitar. This design is suitable for guitars that need to be louder or will be used for strumming, and it's a common design for steel-string guitars. Genres such as rock, folk, and pop often use x-braced guitars.

With fan bracing, several braces fan out from the sound hole. The varied spacing creates a smooth, mellow tone that lends itself to classical music. This bracing system works well with nylon strings.

X-BRACING VS. FAN BRACING

Feature	X-Bracing	Fan Bracing
Sound	Loud and balanced	Warm, mellow, and rich
Best For	Steel-string guitars, strumming	Nylon-string guitars, fingerpicking
Durability	Stronger for more tension	More flexible for less tension
Musical Styles	Folk, pop, country, jazz, alternative	Classical, flamenco, soft genres

PICKGUARD

The pickguard is a protective piece situated on the body of the guitar that protects it from scratches made by guitar picks or fingernails. They're normally made of plastic, but thin layers of metal or wood are also used. This is another piece that's often decorated to add personality to a guitar.

HOW AN ELECTRIC GUITAR WORKS

When you pluck the strings of an electric guitar, something different happens than when you're playing an acoustic. Strumming the strings causes vibrations, but without a hollow body, these sounds are very faint.

Instead, the pickups on electric guitars detect the vibrations, and the wire-wrapped magnets inside each pickup create an electrical signal through a process called *electromagnetic induction*. Once the vibrations are transformed into electrical signals, they travel through wires to the volume and tone controls, then to the output.

The output cable carries the sound to amplifiers, or "amps," where the relatively quiet sounds are made much louder. From there, the amplified electrical signal is sent to speakers that convert it back into sound waves that everyone can enjoy.

ANATOMY OF AN ELECTRIC GUITAR

Electric guitars are very similar to their acoustic counterparts but with a few key differences. In this section, you'll find a brief review of some of the parts we've already discussed, along with more detailed descriptions of the elements unique to electric guitars. Feel free to refer to the previous section for more in-depth descriptions of shared components.

HEADSTOCK

Just like on an acoustic guitar, the headstock is the top part of the neck where the strings connect. That's also the first place you should look for the manufacturer or brand of your guitar.

TUNING PEGS

The headstock is also where the tuning pegs are located. These "machine heads" control the pitch of each string and ensure they stay in tune. The tuning pegs on electric guitars contain the same elements used in acoustic guitars, so you'll find worm gears and string posts here as well.

NUT

Located right below the headstock, the nut is a small piece that runs across the fretboard with small grooves that hold the strings in place. This keeps them evenly spaced and lifted from the fretboard.

STRINGS

Strings on an electric and an acoustic guitar look similar, but they're slightly different. Electric guitar strings are traditionally thinner since they don't rely on thickness to create sound. They're also generally left uncoated to avoid interference with the magnetic response.

Electric guitar strings are made of materials such nickel or steel, which are vital for creating magnetic signals to generate volume through pickups. Using the wrong strings on your guitar may result in poor sound quality, so pay attention when you make a purchase.

NECK

Just like on acoustic guitars, the strings run down the neck, which holds the frets and position markers.

FRETBOARD

The fretboard is the flat surface on the neck that holds everything in place. This is where you push to raise the pitch of your strings.

FRETS

The thin metal strips running across the neck are the frets. Like any guitar, pressing the string near a fret changes how the string vibrates to create the correct pitch. Each fret moves the pitch by half a step, getting higher as you move up.

POSITION MARKERS

This "map" on the neck comes in many styles of design and indicates where the octave of each string is located. They might be dots, squares, or something completely unique.

TRUSS ROD

The truss rod is made of metal and runs down the center of the neck to provide stability. This rod can be adjusted as needed to accommodate various environmental factors.

NECK JOINT

While electric guitars can use the same neck joints as acoustics, bolt-on neck joints are most commonly employed on electric guitars. They're cost effective and easier to repair, and the bright, punchy sound they produce is desirable.

BODY

Just like acoustic guitars, electric guitars are made of wood. However, the body of an electric guitar can be solid, completely hollow, or semi-hollow. The body type you need will depend on what features you're looking for.

Body types affect the guitar's sustain, resonance, and strength of vibration. *Sustain* refers to how long a note resonates; the more sustain, the longer a note can be held.

As the name implies, solid-body guitars are made from a single piece of wood with no sound hole. These are popular for use in rock and metal because of their intense tones and ability to hold up to heavier playing styles. Solid-body guitars reduce energy loss, so they generally produce the most sustain, allowing the notes to continue for longer.

A semi-hollow body has the benefits of both solid and hollow body types. These guitars are made with a solid center and hollow wings. A semi-hollow design generates less feedback than a hollow body, but more than a solid, so it's considered fairly versatile. It provides some sustain and some of the richer tones associated with the hollow body type, making it popular for blues, jazz, and rock.

A hollow body is like an acoustic guitar with a hollow chamber and works well for music that needs less sustain. The downside is that hollow guitars are more likely to produce feedback. The high resonance produced by hollow bodies is good for genres that prefer an acoustic-like sound.

PICKUPS

Situated beneath the strings on the body of an electric guitar, pickups register vibrations and convert them into electrical signals. The magnets in these devices are wrapped with coils of copper wire. This serves to create a magnetic field that moves up and down with the vibrations of the strings. On average, electric guitars contain one to three pickups, and each type of pickup creates a different tone.

PICKUP SELECTOR SWITCH

Some guitars have multiple pickups, each of which produces a different sound. A pickup selector switch allows the guitarist to choose which pickups to use.

KNOBS

Several types of knobs play a role in how the guitar sounds. The volume knob controls the guitar's electrical output to raise or lower the volume. The tone knob adjusts the tone of the sound from warm to bright.

PICKGUARD

Just like on an acoustic guitar, the pickguard protects the body from getting scratched.

BRIDGE

The bridge keeps the strings from disconnecting and transfers vibrations from the strings into the body. Most bridges allow you to adjust the height of the strings to raise or lower the action.

OUTPUT JACK

Perhaps the most important part of the electric guitar, the output jack is where you plug in the cable that connects the guitar to the amplifier. Signals from the various knobs, pickups, and switches all travel to the output jack and through the cable to the amplifier.

CHAPTER TWO: CHOOSING THE RIGHT GUITAR AND TAKING CARE OF IT

As you learn more about the guitar and grow into your skill, you'll be able to play any type of guitar. However, starting out, it's beneficial to focus on one style of guitar and truly master it.

Additionally, once you've chosen your preferred guitar, you'll need to understand how to take care of it. Maintenance is an important part of making sure that your instrument stays in tip-top shape.

FAMOUS BUILDERS, COMPANIES, AND INVENTORS

ANTONIO DE TORRES JURADO

Antonio de Torres Jurado (1817–1892) is considered the father of the modern guitar. He introduced fan bracing, which enabled increased volume and tone projection. His design is the classic template you see in most guitars today.

CHRISTIAN FREDERICK MARTIN

Christian Frederick Martin (1796–1873) was a German luthier who immigrated to the U.S. and founded C. F. Martin & Co. in 1833. While still in Europe, Martin apprenticed under Johann Stauffer, a renowned Viennese guitar maker.

In 1839, Martin relocated his business to Nazareth, Pennsylvania, where it remains there to this day. He became well known for novel guitar designs that combined European construction with American innovations.

Martin developed the x-bracing design, replacing the traditional fan bracing to make the guitar more durable. Another famous Martin design is the Dreadnought, named after a British battleship, which was made with a larger body for increased volume. This design eventually became the default guitar shape.

Moving away from the gut strings that guitars had used for many years, Martin created guitars that could hold up to steel strings. The use of steel strings quickly became the industry standard. He also changed the range. At the time, most guitars had 12 frets, but Martin expanded this to introduce 14 frets. Folk music's popularity cemented Martin's reputation and popularity.

Today, C. F. Martin & Co. remains a family-owned company, producing some of the most popular acoustic guitars available. Martin guitar has been an important player in guitars for 200 years.

ORVILLE GIBSON

Orville Gibson was born in Chateaugay, New York, in 1856, though little is known about his early life. Eventually, he moved to Kalamazoo, Michigan, where he began to experiment with instruments. Unlike many guitar makers, Gibson had no formal luthier training and instead relied on his natural gifts.

In 1894, Gibson created a small workshop in Kalamazoo, where he focused on mandolins, which were popular at the time. He created unique mandolins with a solid wood back and top in the style of violins.

By 1902, this unique design drew the attention of investors, and the Gibson Mandolin-Guitar Manufacturing Company, Ltd., was established. Initially, the company focused on mandolins and archtop guitars.

Gibson stepped back and allowed trained luthiers to work on and improve his designs. In 1922, Gibson introduced the L-5 archtop guitar, a major innovation with a carved spruce top and elevated fretboard, which made it perfect for jazz.

Orville Gibson passed in 1918, but his company lived on. In 1936, the company introduced the ES-150, one of the first commercially successful electric guitars. Gibson is still a cornerstone of guitar manufacturing and remains a legacy to Orville Gibson's memory.

GEORGE WASHBURN LYON

George Washburn Lyon founded Washburn Guitars in Chicago in 1883. Although the company is somewhat less iconic, their rich history of crafting stringed instruments like ukuleles, banjos, and guitars gained them a reputation for producing high-quality instruments.

They ventured into the electric guitar market to expand their ring of influence in the 1970s, and around that time, they started importing from Japan. However, it wasn't until 2012 that they shut down their Illinois factory and moved the rest of their production overseas.

CLARENCE LEONIDAS FENDER

Founded in 1946 by Clarence Leonidas "Leo" Fender in Fullerton, California, Fender Musical Instruments Corporation has become a huge name in the guitar world. Leo was originally a radio repairman but had an interest in all things musical. Because of his technical experience, he was able to tinker with guitars to push the limitations of the instrument.

His first breakthrough came in 1950 with the release of the electric Esquire, a solid guitar with a single pickup. The same year, he improved the model and added a second pickup, christening it the Broadcaster.

Unfortunately, another company manufactured a drum set called Broadkaster, so Fender changed the name to Telecaster. It went on to become the first mass-produced solid-body electric guitar.

In 1954, Fender introduced the Stratocaster, which is recognized as one of the most iconic guitars of all time. With three pickups, a contoured body, and a system allowing players to "bend" the sound, this unique creation is considered one of a kind.

WHAT KIND OF GUITAR WORKS FOR YOU?

While some people lean strongly toward acoustic or electric guitars, others just enjoy playing music, no matter which instrument they use.

SIZING

Along with the decision of what kind of guitar to play, there are also other considerations like size. If your instrument is too large, you'll struggle to reach with your hands and will have to keep your arms unnaturally high.

Most adults can handle a full-size guitar, but don't be scared to look at a smaller instrument if you have short arms or a petite build. Kids ages 4 to 6 can use a 1/4 size guitar, ages 7 to 9 can use a 1/2 size guitar, and kids 10 and up can use a 3/4 size guitar until they're ready for a full-size model.

If you aren't sure what size guitar is right for you, consider your height and arm length; most people over five feet tall can wield a full-size guitar. If you decide you need a smaller guitar, a travel guitar or short guitar may be a good option.

Most electric guitars are narrower than acoustic guitars, so it's easier to find the correct size in electric if you need a smaller option.

PRICE POINT

While your first guitar doesn't need to be a big name in guitars, avoid selecting something at the bottom of the barrel that won't hold up or retain its resale value. Budget guitars can cost under $200 and work just fine for beginners.

At this price point, quality may be inconsistent, but that's not as big an issue while you're learning the basics. A Yamaha F310 (acoustic) or a Squier Bullet Stratocaster (electric) are both great options for a beginner on a budget.

Once you're comfortable enough to look for an upgrade, check out instruments in the $200 to $500 range. The Yamaha FG800 (acoustic) has great tone and holds up well, and the Squier Classic Vibe Series (electric) is another affordable option.

Once you start perfecting your art, you might want to invest in a nicer guitar in the $500 to $1,000 range. The Breedlove Pursuit Concert (acoustic) is a versatile instrument with unique tone, while the Fender Player Series Stratocaster (electric) is characterized by the classic sound Fender is known for.

If you decide to play professionally, specialty guitars can cost anywhere from $1,000 to $2,000. The Gibson G-45 Studio (acoustic) and the Fender American Professional II Stratocaster/Telecaster (electric) are both designed for recording and professional performances.

While some guitars range over $2,000, these are appropriate for collectors or extremely experienced players. While they offer better sound and tone, big investments like these are better suited to enthusiasts. However, if you're interested, look at the Martin D-28 or ESP E-II FRX FM, which both retail around $2,800.

The most expensive guitars can cost over $100,000. The Martin Limited Edition D-200 Deluxe retails for around $135,000.

ALL TYPES OF GUITARS

Although electric and acoustic are the most widely known types of guitars, variations on these designs are also popular with some musicians.

- **Bass:** Bass guitars are built specifically to produce low-frequency tones that are essential for rhythm in many music genres. A bass guitar can either be electric or acoustic.
- **Archtop:** This type of guitar is hollow with an arched top. It's often used in jazz and blues, and it comes in both acoustic and electric versions.
- **Resonator:** A resonator is an acoustic guitar that lacks a traditional sound hole. Instead, it uses a metal resonator cone with a very distinct sound. Resonators are most commonly used in blues and bluegrass music.
- **Classical:** Classical guitars are wide-necked instruments with nylon strings that are frequently used for classical and flamenco music.
- **Twelve-string:** Instead of the traditional six strings, twelve-string guitars have twice as many and produce a rich tone.
- **Baritone:** These guitars have longer scale lengths and are tuned lower than the average guitar, giving them a deeper tonal range.

WOOD USED FOR GUITARS

The wood that a guitar is made of can have a huge impact on the resonance and tone of the instrument. For instance, some woods create warmer tones, while others lean toward a brighter, punchier sound. Each different wood has its own benefits and drawbacks, but one of the biggest deciding factors is the amount of sustain each wood provides.

ALDER

With balanced tone, good sustain, and clear highs, alder is a good wood for many different genres. It's lightweight and good for playing over extended periods. Plus, alder is often chosen for its tonal consistency.

However, while it can be a great choice, alder isn't as pretty as some other woods. It's also softer than other options, so it might be damaged more easily.

ASH

Ash wood provides a balanced tone within the midrange, good sustain, and clear highs. It's both versatile and lightweight, which makes it a good choice for extended performance. Ash is great for genres like country or funk.

In addition to being practical, ash is a beautiful wood. The open grain pattern makes this wood popular for aesthetic reasons. Swamp ash is particularly ideal for transparent finishes.

Because it's a denser wood, ash can be harder to work with. Some varieties are fairly rare, making those types of ash less cost effective.

MAHOGANY

Mahogany wood gives guitars a rich, warm tone with good sustain that's well suited to lower frequencies. Although it's a heavier wood, the sustain and resonance it provides make the extra weight worth it.

While popular for genres like blues, rock, and jazz, overharvesting has made mahogany a more expensive option.

MAPLE

Maple is a dense wood that creates a very articulated tone and good sustain. Because of its heavy weight, maple is rarely used for the body of the guitar but is commonly used for neck and tops.

When paired with other woods, maple can provide tonal clarity and visual appeal. However, maple pieces can make guitars more expensive.

BASSWOOD

A good midrange wood with no extreme highs or lows, basswood is lightweight and easy to handle. It's a common material in budget-friendly and mid-tier guitars.

The downside of this soft wood is a tendency to get damaged, especially since the genres it works best for are shredding and rock. Some guitarists say that basswood lacks depth, and its bland grain doesn't work well for transparent finishes.

ROSEWOOD

Rosewood is ideal for fretboards because of its natural harmonic overtones. Rosewood adds a luxurious feel and smooth playing for an overall warmer tone.

However, the wood is extremely heavy, which means it isn't used for the body. Additionally, overharvesting has led to restrictions on its use, so it can be expensive.

Rosewood is naturally oily, which complicates the manufacturing process, but this also gives it a soft, natural feel. Overall, rosewood is great for fretboards but not for the whole guitar.

EBONY

If you need a guitar with a bright, snappy tone, look for a guitar with an ebony fretboard. Guitars with ebony fretwork have a luxurious feel and sound that works well for fast-playing musicians.

While it's extremely durable, ebony is very expensive and in high demand. Because of unsustainable practices, this wood is hard to find and even harder to ethically source.

If you do manage to get your hands on some ebony, make sure you maintain it by oiling; it's prone to drying out, which leads to cracking.

POPLAR

While similar to alder in balance, poplar produces a warmer tone with less resonance. Poplar is common in beginner guitars because of its budget-friendly price point. It's also an extremely reliable, lightweight wood, which works great for mass production.

The downside to poplar material is that it's not the prettiest of woods. Although technically a hardwood, it's on the softer side, which means it's prone to dents and scratches.

KORINA

Korina, also known as white limba, has a resonant tone and rich harmonies. Korina has beautiful wood grain patterns, but it isn't a commonly seen wood. Guitars made of korina have a very niche appeal.

Korina wood has been used in several iconic guitars like Gibson's Flying V. This extremely rare, expensive wood can be challenging to work with and resists machine finishing, which further adds to the cost.

SPRUCE

A popular wood for acoustic guitars, spruce has a crisp tone and stays clear across a wide range of frequencies. Whether the guitarist is playing soft or hard, spruce provides a solid sustain.

This light wood is ideal for longer performances and works well for many genres. It's also visually appealing, which isn't as common in lighter woods.

However, like many lighter woods, spruce needs to be taken care of to prevent scratching. Because of its lack of density, it's only used in hollow guitars.

Depending on the variety of spruce, the price tag can sometimes run high, but for the most part, it's a solid wood with a good price point.

CEDAR

Great for acoustic guitars, cedar creates a warm, rich tone and does well in the midrange. This lightweight wood is often used for the tops of classical and fingerstyle acoustic guitars because it's so responsive and warm.

Cedar is softer than spruce, making it easy to scratch, and its smaller range and lack of projection make it less than ideal for large venues.

EQUIPMENT FOR ACOUSTIC AND ELECTRIC GUITARS

As you learn to play the guitar, some equipment will help you along the way. Once you're an accomplished player, you'll want a few more accessories as well.

TUNERS

A tuner is used to check the pitch of your strings and make sure your guitar is in tune. Below, we've listed several different types of tuners, but other options are available, depending on what you consider most convenient.

Clip-on tuners are popular for their ease of use and convenience. The clip-on attaches to the headstock of a guitar and registers the vibration on the strings. Powered with batteries and often rechargeable, clip-on tuners work well in loud environments that might interfere with other tuners.

Designed exclusively for electric guitars, pedal tuners are larger than clip-ons and run on DC power. Pedal tuners sit on the ground, ideally on a pedalboard, for a hands-free option. They're more accurate and mute the electric signal while in use so that the audience can't hear you tuning.

Handheld tuners are small and portable, making them convenient for travel. They're battery operated, which makes them useful in any situation, and they often have a screen that's easy to read in many lighting conditions. Some versions come with options for both plug-in tuning for electric guitars and a built-in microphone for acoustics.

Other types of tuners include phone apps and, if you're feeling nostalgic, an old-fashioned pitch pipe. A good starting tuner is the Snark SN5X, a budget-friendly clip-on.

CAPOS

Have you ever noticed a clamp across the neck of a guitar? These are called *capos*, and they work by holding down the strings at a chosen fret, shortening the length of all the strings. This raises the pitch without the need to change fingering.

Capos make playing in different keys easier so that you can transpose songs and play a wider range of music. Once you start learning how to play the guitar, you'll understand the benefits of having a wider musical range without having to change the way you play.

For a beginner-friendly capo, consider the Kyser Quick-Change Capo, which is spring loaded for easy repositioning.

GUITAR STRAPS

No matter what kind of guitar you choose, a guitar strap is a handy accessory. These straps run across your shoulder to hold your guitar while you play. When you're playing for longer periods of time, it's a useful tool for keeping the weight off your arms.

Guitar straps are also a great way to customize your guitar because they come in tons of styles and colors. They also allow you to express yourself by giving you the freedom to move while playing.

Guitar straps can be made of various materials. Nylon is a lightweight and durable option, and leather is stylish and long lasting. Some straps are even padded for extra comfort. A quality nylon strap costs about $10 to $20, while leather straps can run over $50.

When you're strap shopping, consider the width of the band and try different straps until you find one that sits comfortably on your shoulder.

PICKS

A pick can be used both to strum your guitar and play individual notes, providing a more consistent sound than your fingers while protecting them from injury. Picks have been used with stringed instruments for thousands of years.

Historically, picks were made of stone, bone, tortoiseshell, or even feather quills. Starting in the early twentieth century, companies like Fender started producing plastic picks and discovered that they were cheaper and durable. Although plastic is the most popular material, picks are still made from other materials like metal and wood, which offer a range of different sounds.

The teardrop shape of standard guitar picks works well for all styles of playing, but some specialty picks come in different shapes and thicknesses. For example, jazz picks are smaller and pointier, while thumb picks attach to your thumb and leave your fingers free to pluck the strings.

When you get ready to buy your first pick, start with a variety pack so that you can try different types to find your best match. Once you learn which kind of pick works for you, you may want to find a custom pick that you like the look of along with the feel.

GUITAR STANDS

When you aren't playing, a guitar stand is a handy tool to set your guitar down quickly. It's convenient for use during gigs to make sure your guitar doesn't get scratched or damaged without having to stow it in your case.

A guitar stand also allows you to easily grab your instrument whenever you want to play. Having your guitar within reach will no doubt encourage you to practice and play more.

Additionally, a guitar stand is the perfect place to display your guitar like the work of art it is. Whether you have a generic guitar or a custom, one-of-a-kind piece, you should be proud of your burgeoning skill. Seeing your guitar might even inspire you to visit places like the Songbird Guitar and Pop Culture Museum in Chattanooga, Tennessee, where you can view a variety of rare and vintage guitars.

One of the most common stand designs is the tripod, which is generally recommended for beginners. As the name suggests, these stands have three feet. They're fairly stable, especially because the tripod feet support a pole with a cradle for the guitar's neck. Although some tripod stands feature collapsible designs, they're not very portable; luckily, that shouldn't be a problem when you're starting out.

A-frame stands, on the other hand, are simple and portable with just two legs and wide feet. A hook to hold the guitar's body makes it suitable for both electric and acoustic guitars. The downside to A-frame stands is their relative instability. Because they lack a neck cradle, your guitar is likely to fall over if bumped.

If you don't have much space to display your guitar, try using a hanging stand to display your guitar on the wall. You can also find stands for more than one guitar as your collection grows.

Whichever stand you decide to use, make sure it fits your guitar and has plenty of padding in addition to a sturdy base. Stands can be very budget friendly, starting at around $15, but fancy ones can cost you hundreds of dollars. Custom stands can even range into the thousands, but unless you're an avid collector, a budget stand can do the job just as well as more expensive options.

GUITAR CASES

A guitar stand is fine while you're in one place, but it's important to have a way to transport your guitar safely — and this is where a guitar case comes into play. Guitar cases are used to carry and store your guitar and protect it from damage. Since most guitar cases come with pockets and compartments, they're also handy for storing accessories.

Guitar cases are another way to show your personality and customize your guitar's look. Because the knobs and switches on electric guitars are magnets for dust, it's especially important to store them in a case.

Cases come in many styles, but the main difference is whether the case is hard or soft. Soft cases, or "gig bags," are made from synthetic material and heavily padded. They're great for short trips because they're lightweight with straps like a backpack.

Hard cases are better for longer trips or situations where you won't be carrying your guitar much or you're concerned it might be damaged. Hard cases are made of rigid materials such as wood, plastic, or fiberglass. High-end cases can even be made of carbon fiber, which is durable and lightweight.

In situations like flying when your guitar might be tossed around, you'll want a hard case with metal reinforcement and a lock. To prevent security from prying open your case and possibly damaging it, make sure to use a TSA-approved lock.

While soft cases can be water resistant, some hard cases are completely waterproof. There are also hybrid cases that combine different elements to suit your needs. If you find yourself in need of something specific, custom options are available.

When buying a case, make sure it's designed for the type of guitar you have. Look for padding that will hold up to your lifestyle. No matter what you need, you can choose from price points ranging anywhere from $50 to several hundred.

STRING WINDERS AND CUTTERS

Guitar strings endure a lot of abuse from vibrations, exposure to the oil in your skin, and atmospheric conditions. Some players need to replace their strings more often, and you'll be able to tell when the sound starts changing. You'll get more time out of your strings if you take care of them and store your guitar properly.

Even with the utmost care, however, strings corrode over time. When it's time to change your strings, string winders and cutters make the job easier. Winders quickly turn the tuning pegs to wrap the string, and cutters allow you to remove the excess.

Even if you don't have a winder or cutter, you can still replace your guitar's strings yourself. However, twisting the strings by hand can lead to finger strain, and it's time consuming. If you're nervous about doing it yourself, most stores will replace your strings for you, though they'll likely charge a service fee.

AMPLIFIERS

Amplifiers increase the volume of electric guitars and shape the sound with bass, treble, and other effects. The amp is a pivotal tool, whether you're on stage playing to an audience or settled in your living room for a personal jam.

The first guitar amps came into use in the 1930s, but technology has improved drastically since the turn of the century due to digital processing power. While technology continues to evolve, the physical parts of the amp remain largely the same. Amps are stored in cabinets with a speaker inside, and even though compact options are available, all amps take up space.

The larger a speaker, the better it will be at producing low tones. Similarly, smaller speakers are better at producing high tones. One of the most common sizes for amps is right in the midrange at 12 inches.

When choosing an amp, pick a size that makes sense with the venue you'll be playing most often. Take your guitar with you when you go shopping so that you can try each amp before you make a purchase.

TUBE AMPLIFIERS

This is the oldest type of amp. It works by utilizing glass vacuum tubes. Tube amps are well known for producing a warm, smooth sound, and they're especially popular among musicians aiming for a "classic" sound.

Because the tubes are fragile, they need to be replaced often, which can get expensive. Unless you have the budget, other options might suit you better. Despite the cost of maintaining tube amps, many believe they provide the best sound.

SOLID-STATE AMPLIFIERS

In the mid-twentieth century, solid-state amps arrived on the market. These amps use transistors or semiconductor circuits rather than tubes, making them lightweight, cost effective, and more reliable than tube amps.

Because they can achieve higher volumes without distortion, solid-state amps are considered perfect for jazz and other genres that value clean tones. While they lack the warmth of tube amps, solid-state amps are much easier to maintain, making them a popular option for many musicians.

DIGITAL AMPLIFIERS

Newest on the scene, digital amps use cutting-edge technology to deliver flexibility with a variety of sound. Despite their versatility and ease of use, some still prefer the more organic sound of analog models.

PEDALBOARDS

While pedals aren't necessary for a guitar to create beautiful music, they do allow for experimentation with sound and tone. Guitar pedals have been around since the early 1940s when the DeArmond Tremolo Control was introduced. This unit featured a knob that could be moved up and down to create a wavering effect.

In 1961, a damaged preamplifier created a fuzzy tone during the recording of Marty Robbins's "Don't Worry." This interesting new sound became popular, leading to the design of one of the first commercially successful, mass-produced pedals—the Maestro Fuzz-Tone—in 1962. This iconic sound can be heard at the beginning of "(I Can't Get No) Satisfaction" by the Rolling Stones.

Guitar pedals continued to gain popularity, creating such effects as distortion, pitch variations, and modulation. "Wah" pedals are designed to mimic human speech, as is the more versatile "talk box."

Despite their name, pedals aren't exclusively controlled by foot. Many pedals include hand-adjustable knobs to control their effects. Pedals also require an output, so they can only be used with electronic instruments.

COMMONLY USED PEDALS

Pedals allow for endless creativity, and you can use multiple pedals for even more range. As you gain more experience, you may want to consider using these types of pedals:

- **Chorus:** Chorus pedals create the illusion of multiple instruments playing at once, adding richness to the music.
- **Distortion and overdrive:** These pedals are used primarily in rock and metal. Distortion pedals create a gritty sound.
- **Looper:** Looper pedals allow you to record a section of music and repeat it while you move on to the next riff.
- **Wah:** Often used for funk and blues, this pedal creates a *wah* sound that mimics vocalization.
- **Delay and reverb:** These pedals add various echo effects. Delay repeats the original sound, while reverb simulates the natural reverberations of a large space.

Once you collect a few pedals, you should consider organizing them on a pedalboard. Without one, pedals can slide out of place at inconvenient times and their cords may become tangled and difficult to use.

CLEANING AND MAINTENANCE SUPPLIES

If you want your guitar to have a long life, regular maintenance and cleaning is important. To keep your instrument in tip-top shape, you'll need a few supplies. Make sure you follow any instructions that come with your guitar and speak to a professional if you have any questions.

A high-quality polish can help maintain a glossy finish by removing the oil, dust, and grime that will inevitably build up. However, polish can damage matte or satin finishes, so make sure to check the care instructions for your guitar.

You should also consider keeping a fretboard conditioner in your bag to keep your fretboard from drying out. Dry wood is often prone to cracks and "fret sprout," a condition caused by shrinking wood where the frets protrude beyond the edges of the fretboard. A hydrated fretboard has a nicer feel and look.

Even if you keep your instrument as clean as possible, your strings will eventually need cleaning. String cleaner removes oil and dirt that builds up over time, ensuring your strings last for as long as possible.

When you're shopping for guitar cleaning products, make sure to choose quality over quantity. You won't need a lot, but it's important to use products that won't harm your guitar.

CLEANING AN ACOUSTIC GUITAR

One of the best ways to keep your guitar clean is to wash your hands before you play and wipe down your guitar after every use. While these steps will help you avoid the need for heavy cleaning, all guitars need regular maintenance.

Microfiber cloth works well for cleaning, but any soft fabric will work. You should also use a specialty cleaner made for the specific material of your guitar.

FRETBOARD

Anytime you change your strings, you should clean your fretboard as well. Use a fretboard conditioner regularly to clean and hydrate it.

Lemon oil is a great conditioner for keeping wood from cracking. Oil shouldn't be used on finished fretboards, though, so double check your guitar's maintenance instructions before applying anything.

STORAGE

Another factor to consider is the ideal level of humidity for guitar storage. Between 40 and 60 percent humidity is best for wooden guitars because it helps prevent warping, cracking, and drying of the wood. In extremely dry climates, putting a humidifier in your guitar storage space is an excellent idea.

On the other hand, too much moisture can cause swelling, which is just as bad. If you live in an area with high humidity, keeping a dehumidifier near your guitar is recommended.

TUNING

Make sure to tune your guitar regularly, especially during seasonal changes. Fluctuations in temperature can lead to shifts in your guitar's sound. String tension can also change as the atmosphere warms and cools, causing strain on the neck.

Tuning your guitar involves adjusting the tuning pegs until the string hits the right note. If the pitch is too low, or flat, turn the tuning peg counterclockwise to raise the pitch. If your note is too high, or sharp, turning the peg clockwise will lower the pitch.

You can tune your guitar with an electrical tuner or by matching pitch with another instrument. Tuning to a piano or pitch pipe is good practice for familiarizing yourself with the sound of each note.

Once you get one string in tune, you can use that string to adjust the others, which makes tuning faster and easier; it also ensures that each string is in tune with the others. After tuning the first string, put a finger behind the fifth fret of the second string and adjust it to match. For the third string, put a finger behind the fourth fret and adjust the peg until they sound the same, then continue until every string is in tune.

HARDWARE

Make sure that you're regularly checking for issues with the various pieces of your guitar. This should include inspecting the tuning pegs, bridge, strap button, fretboard, and so on.

When you find an issue, handle it right away or take it to a professional. Over time, a poorly maintained guitar will stop producing its best-quality music.

If you ever feel like you're in over your head, visit your local music shop. There will be someone who can help you and guide you along your guitar journey. In any case, having a professional examine your guitar every few years is a good idea.

ACOUSTIC GUITAR CARE CHECKLIST:

- Wash your hands thoroughly before playing.
- Wipe your guitar after every use.
- Replace strings as needed.
- Store in a safe place.
- Monitor the humidity levels.
- Avoid extreme temperature fluctuations.
- Tune frequently.
- Regularly check for any issues.
- Visit a professional for a deep check.

CLEANING AN ELECTRIC GUITAR

Most of the maintenance an electric guitar requires will be the same as an acoustic, but there are a few differences. Obviously, you should wipe your electric guitar down after every use and clean it regularly with a cleaner designed for your specific guitar. The metal elements on electric guitars can be polished with a soft cloth to keep them shiny and prevent rust.

ELECTRONICS

Since electronics are the soul of electronic guitars, it's crucial to keep them in good condition. Like all electronics, your guitar won't get along well with liquids, so make sure to protect it from moisture.

Electric guitars also have more nooks and crannies than acoustics. It's important to keep dust or dirt from accumulating. Wiping down your guitar regularly will help, but occasionally you might need a deeper clean.

Try using a contact cleaner like DeoxIT on a pipe cleaner or a mascara brush to clean small areas. A cotton swab will work in a pinch, but make sure it doesn't come apart and leave bits of fiber behind. Rubbing alcohol will also work because it evaporates quickly. While compressed air is another option, be careful—the cans can sometimes leak condensed liquid, which can damage your finish or electronics.

STORAGE

You should follow all the same rules when storing an electric or an acoustic guitar: Avoid extreme temperatures, humidity, and unnecessary roughness. You should also avoid storing your guitar for long periods of time whenever possible. Guitars improve in sound the more they're played, following a process that's called "playing in."

TUNING

When you don't play your guitar regularly, string tension can damage the neck over time. If you plan to store your guitar for more than a few months, consider loosening the strings a half or full step to prevent bowing. If your guitar has a truss rod, you'll need to adjust it to a neutral position as well.

HARDWARE

Do a visual check regularly to look for any potential or emerging problems. Fix issues as soon as you run across them to prevent them from getting worse. An occasional visit to a professional is also a good idea.

ELECTRIC GUITAR CARE CHECKLIST:

- Wash your hands thoroughly before playing.
- Wipe the guitar after every use.
- Change strings as needed.
- Keep the electronics dust free.

- Stored in correct temperature and humidity.
- Tune before playing.
- Check for loose screws or knobs.
- Visit a professional.

STRINGS

As a rule of thumb, you should plan to replace your guitar strings every few months or after 100 hours of playing. New strings always sound the best because they're free of oil and grime, which can impede the vibrations of the string. The more you play, the more often you'll need to change your strings.

Of course, cleaning your strings will also extend their life. While some strings can be boiled, others require string cleaner, so always check the care instructions. Wiping down your strings every time you play will keep them cleaner, and there are also special tools that help you clean your strings.

With the wide selection of strings available, you may want to try several different types to find what works best for you. The right strings improve sound quality, bringing new life to your guitar.

Replace your strings when any of them are broken, the tension isn't working, or the sound has changed. Some professional guitarists even change strings before every performance to ensure the highest possible sound quality.

REPLACING STRINGS

The first step is to make sure you understand which direction to turn the pegs to loosen them and release the strings. Usually, one side turns clockwise and the other counterclockwise.

Loosen the pegs completely and remove the strings, then insert the new string into the bridge pin and gently tighten to remove slack. Once you've done this, wrap the new string about the peg several times. Finally, trim the excess with a string cutter if you like.

CHECKING NUTS

The nut that holds the strings in place is a vital element of your guitar. If you're having trouble tuning your guitar, it's possible that the nut is too high.

When checking your nut, the first step is to clean any accumulated dirt from dead skin and sweat, which can work its way up the strings to the nut. Once you've removed the strings, you can clean the slots in the nut.

If cleaning doesn't resolve the problem, it's time to repair the nut by smoothing out the slot. Nut files are a handy tool for this, but a triangular nail file will also do the trick.

After smoothing the slot, coat the area with lead from a graphite pencil to lubricate the strings. If you don't want to use a pencil, specialized string lubricants are available.

You can always take your guitar to a specialist if cleaning doesn't fix the problem. Sometimes a new nut needs to be installed, but usually, repairing the nut is an easy fix.

CHAPTER THREE: BUILDING YOUR FOUNDATION

While much of traditional music theory focuses on piano and orchestral music, you'll need to understand the essentials and what makes the guitar unique.

GETTING COMFORTABLE WITH YOUR GUITAR

In order to grow more comfortable with your guitar, it's important to learn the proper way to hold it, which features you'll use the most, and how to keep your instrument in good shape.

HOW TO HOLD YOUR GUITAR

Although it may seem counterintuitive, you should use a strap even when you're seated. Begin by sitting in a comfortable position on a stool or chair. Depending on your personal preference, either leave your legs open or cross them.

If you leave your legs open, try to elevate your dominant leg; if you cross them, have your dominant leg on top. If your seat doesn't allow you to raise your leg into the correct posture, consider using a footstool designed to raise your leg and support the guitar comfortably.

Rest your guitar on the same leg as your dominant hand. The guitar should hit just below the chest with your back completely straight. Use your dominant hand to strum while your other hand works the frets.

As you play, tuck the guitar loosely under your elbow. Your dominant hand should drape comfortably over the body of the guitar, resting halfway over the sound hole. If your elbow feels too high, the guitar might be too large for you.

The guitar should tilt upward slightly, but not everyone finds the same angle comfortable. Feel free to lower the neck if you're uncomfortable, but keep it angled at least 20 degrees up to avoid straining your wrist. The hand working the frets needs to be relaxed but strong, running under the guitar at a 90-degree angle without bending your wrist.

Everyone has different preferences, so play around until you find your preferred position. There are no hard and fast rules as long as you're comfortable enough to play for extended periods of time.

LEARNING YOUR FRETBOARD

Most acoustic guitars have 20 frets, while electrics can have up to 24. Each fret represents a note along the string. When you push on the strings to create music, press down in the space between the frets rather than directly on them. For instance, when someone talks about the fifth fret, they actually mean the space in front of it.

On your fretboard, you'll notice symbols marking the third, fifth, seventh, ninth, and twelfth frets. The mark at the twelfth fret stands out from the rest to indicate the next octave. After that point, the symbols repeat at similar intervals.

STANDARD TUNING

Six strings run across your fretboard, starting with the lowest and thickest string. The strings represent the notes E, A, D, G, and B, with the last string repeating E but an octave higher. The highest string is often denoted with a lowercase e to avoid confusion. The strings are often referred to by numbers instead of letters, running thickest to thinnest (i.e., sixth, fifth, fourth, third, second, and first).

This is considered standard tuning. A good way to remember those notes is with this acrostic:

Eddie

Ate

Dynamite

Good

Bye

Eddie

MORE MUSICAL NOTES ON THE FRETBOARD

The process of learning to play any instrument begins with understanding notes and scales, and guitar is no exception. To this end, you'll need to become familiar with the intervals on the fretboard and the notes they represent. Moving a half step up from a note makes it sharp ($\#$), while a half step down makes it flat ($\flat$). For example, the next fret up from G is G$\#$, while the fret below is G$\flat$.

Some notes are the same pitch, but they're notated differently. For example, G$\#$ and A$\flat$ sound the same, but how they're written depends on which key the music is set in. These notes are called *enharmonic equivalents*, and their notation is determined by context.

There are some variations, however; for instance, B and C are only a half step apart, so B$\#$ is actually equivalent to C, not C$\flat$.

THE BASICS OF PLAYING NOTES AND SCALES

All music is composed of notes that are organized into scales that repeat at regular intervals called *octaves*. While you don't necessarily need to get super technical, understanding the basics is important for any musician.

OCTAVES

To play guitar, you push the strings at certain points on your fretboard, but when a string is played without pressing down at any of the frets, it's considered *open*.

There are a total of 12 notes in each octave. After that, the notes start repeating at a higher octave. The thirteenth fret is an octave higher than the first fret, the fourteenth fret is an octave higher than the second fret, and so on.

It's important to memorize these corresponding octaves, as you'll use them your entire guitar career.

1st	13th
2nd	14th
3rd	15th
4th	16th
5th	17th
6th	18th
7th	19th

8th	20th

SCALES

Scales are patterns of musical notes played in a specific sequence. Practicing scales improves your dexterity, playing strength, and improvisation ability while creating muscle memory. Playing scales also helps guitarists become familiar with the fretboard. With time, you'll get used to the sounds your guitar makes, helping you develop a musical ear.

Some scales are also known as *modes*, but all come in various forms, each evoking a different feeling. However, all scales begin with a root and end at the next octave. Most scales contain seven notes (or eight, if you count the octave). Below, we've compiled the most common scales that you need to master.

MAJOR SCALE

The major scale evokes a feeling of happiness and follows a set pattern of whole and half steps:

R–W–W–H–W–W–W–H

(R = root, W = whole step, H = half step)

A common example is the C major scale:

C–D–E–F–G–A–B–C

MINOR SCALE

Also called "natural" minor, these types of scales are generally associated with sadness or solemnity. The pattern of whole and half steps in the minor scale looks like this:

W–H–W–W–H–W–W

A good example of a minor scale is A minor:

A–B–C–D–E–F–G–A

MODES

Modes set the tone of music, evoking different emotions within the listener. A mode is a type of musical scale built using natural notes with no sharps or flats. Depending on which note the scale begins with, modes can summon a variety of feelings. For example, what you know as the major scale is also Ionian mode, while natural minor is the same as Aeolian mode.

There are seven modes for each major scale: Ionian (major), Dorian, Phrygian, Lydian, Mixolydian, Aeolian (natural minor), and Locrian.

	The Seven Modes	
Mode Name	Starting Note (Using C Major as an Example)	Sound/Mood
Ionian (Major)	C–D–E–F–G–A–B–C	Bright, happy, uplifting
Dorian	D-E–F–G–A-B-C-D	Jazzy, bluesy, mysterious
Phrygian	E–F–G–A–B-C–D–E	Dark, exotic
Lydian	F-G-A–B–C–D-E-F	Dreamy, floating, open
Mixolydian	G–A–B–C–D-E-F-G	Bluesy, rebellious
Aeolian (Natural Minor)	A–B–C–D-E–F–G–A	Sad, solemn, moody
Locrian	B-C-D-E-F-G-A-B	Dissonant, unstable, tense

PENTATONIC SCALE

A great tool for composing solos and one of the most popular scales for guitarists, pentatonic scales are often heard in rock and blues music. A pentatonic scale has five notes rather than the typical seven.

Pentatonic scales come in major or minor and are quick and easy to learn. Simply remove the fourth and seventh of a major scale and play the first, second, third, fifth, and sixth notes. A minor pentatonic scale is also an abbreviated version of its counterpart, using the first, flat third (♭ 3), fourth, fifth, and flat seventh (♭ 7) notes of a minor scale.

An example of the pentatonic scale is the E minor pentatonic scale:

$$E–G–A–B–D–E$$

Another pentatonic scale is A minor:

$$A–C–D–E–G–A$$

BLUES SCALE

The blues scale is easy to learn once you've mastered pentatonic scale because it's just a minor pentatonic scale with an additional flattened fifth that creates a bluesy sound.

An example of a blues scale is the A blues scale:

$$A–C–D–D\sharp–E–G–A$$

USING CAPOS EFFECTIVELY

The capo is a great tool for new and experienced guitarists alike because it makes changing keys possible without complicating the fingering. It works by clamping the strings to shorten them and raise their pitch. For example, if you place a capo on the second fret and position your fingers for a C chord, you'll actually produce a D chord.

There are several reasons for using a capo, including making certain songs easier to play, creating new sounds, and transposing a song (changing the key). Transposing a song can be a huge benefit if you intend to sing along with your guitar because you can change the key to fit within your vocal range. It can also be helpful when playing with other artists.

When you put the capo on your guitar, make sure it fits correctly and is balanced on the strings. As long as you're careful, putting a capo on is super easy and fast.

CAPO CHART

Capo charts show you where you need to place your capo to achieve the desired key.

STRUMMING AND PICKING TECHNIQUES

HOW TO STRUM

In order to play chords, you need to know how to work the strings on your guitar. Only the tips of the fingers of your fretting hand should touch the strings. Pushing right behind the fret, as close as you can without touching it. As you press down, keep your fingers as straight as possible so that you don't accidentally touch any of the other strings.

Pushing too hard is referred to as *over-fretting* and causes muted sounds, incorrect notes, damaged strings, and finger fatigue. Use gentle pressure to depress the strings, keeping in mind that thinner strings need less pressure.

Practice fretting each string individually until you're familiar with the amount of pressure needed to get a clear sound with no buzzing. Practicing diligently helps develop muscle memory, and once your fingers are used to playing, it becomes instinctive.

FINGERPICKING

Fingerpicking is a beautiful and expressive way to play the guitar, allowing for more intricate melodies and rhythmic patterns. You'll see this technique a lot in folk, classical, blues, country, and even rock. While strumming limits you to hitting multiple strings at one time, fingerpicking involves plucking each string individually.

One basic pattern is a C major chord played one note at a time: thumb, index, middle, and ring. Fingers are denoted by letters — your thumb is *P*, index is *I*, middle is *M*, and ring finger is *A*. These letters come from the Spanish words for fingers (*pulgar, índice, medio, anular*) and are used in classical guitar notation. Beyond basic fingerpicking, advanced fingerpicking techniques like arpeggios can add a flowing, harp-like quality to your music.

CHAPTER FOUR: MASTERING CHORD PROGRESSIONS AND RHYTHM

RHYTHM AND TIMING

UNDERSTANDING TIME SIGNATURES

Have you ever noticed how certain types of music make you want to jump up and dance, while others inspire you to a slow waltz? This has a lot to do with time signatures. It's important learn about them so that you can play music how it's intended and collaborate with others.

A time signature is a symbol in music notation that indicates the meter, or how many beats are in each measure and what kind of note gets one beat. Time signatures look a lot like fractions and appear at the beginning of each piece. Sometimes, you'll see more than one, indicating a change in meter. The top number lets you know how many beats are in a measure, and the bottom number lets you know what type of note equals one beat.

- **4/4 time:** Four beats per measure, quarter note gets the beat (also known as "common time")
- **3/4 time:** Three beats per measure, quarter note gets the beat ("waltz rhythm")
- **6/8 time:** Six beats per measure, eighth note gets the beat

4 / 4 TIME

This is the most common meter — thus the name "common time" — that's used in many genres. You've probably used the beat even if you didn't realize. You can play this meter by strumming down on the first and third beats for a steady feel or emphasize the second and fourth beats to create a syncopated rhythm.

3 / 4 TIME

You might have noticed a "ONE–two–three" feel in certain slow songs. This waltz rhythm is common in folk, country, and classical music. When you play in this meter, emphasize the first beat and strum lightly on the second and third beats.

6 / 8 TIME

While it may seem like just another way to indicate waltz rhythm, 6/8 time has a completely different feel that's commonly found in blues and ballads. To produce the distinctive rolling rhythm of the 6/8 meter, bring out beats one and four and back off on two, three, five, and six: "ONE–two–three, FOUR–five–six."

Time Signature	Beat Pattern	Example Song	Genre
4/4	1-2-3-4	"Wonderwall" - Oasis	Rock/Pop
3/4	1-2-3	"Piano Man" - Billy Joel	Folk
6/8	1-2-3, 4-5-6	"House of the Rising Sun" - The Animals	Blues/Rock

DOWNSTROKES VS. UPSTROKES

The two basic movements of strumming are distinguished by the direction your hand is moving when it passes over the strings.

DOWNSTROKES: A POWER STRUM

A downstroke moves from top to bottom and rises in pitch. This smooth movement creates a strong, full sound that's perfect for driving a beat. Many punk and rock guitarists use exclusively downstrokes to produce a tight, aggressive sound that makes for powerful songs.

UPSTROKES: A LIGHT TOUCH

An upstroke starts at the bottom and moves up but doesn't generally hit every string. The light sound produced by upstrokes adds subtlety and variety, creating a natural flow to your playing.

Upstrokes create the bouncy, laid-back vibe that reggae is known for. Ska musicians also favor upstrokes and often mute the strings on downstrokes for a percussive feel.

SYNCOPATION AND GROOVE

Syncopation occurs when you play slightly off beat, creating a natural feel. Instead of emphasizing the main beats, syncopation focus on the in-between beats to make the rhythm exciting. Look at it like dancing: If you do the exact same move over and over, it gets boring. Similarly, variation makes music seem more alive.

Groove is the feeling of the music and the rhythm. When you hear music that makes you tap your feet and bop your head, that's groove. When you're playing, keep your hand loose for smooth strumming, concentrate on feeling the beat, and vary your dynamics with upstrokes, downstrokes, and different pressures.

PERCUSSIVE TECHNIQUES

There are other ways to create sound with your guitar beyond simply strumming chords and picking notes. Different styles create rhythm and dynamics with percussive techniques like palm muting. Many genres use these techniques, including rock, punk, funk, and pop.

PALM MUTING

Palm muting involves placing your strumming hand on the strings while you're playing near the bridge of the guitar. This technique prevents the strings from ringing out freely, muffling the sound to make the notes shorter and tighter.

HOW TO PALM MUTE

1. **Position your hand:** Place the side of your fret hand's palm — the fleshy part on your pinky's side — gently on the strings, close to the bridge.
2. **Strum the strings:** Holding your fret hand in place, strum the strings as you normally would.

3. **Adjust the pressure:** If the resulting sound is too quiet, you're using too much pressure, so you need to lighten up. When the notes don't sound muffled enough, you need to push harder.

Bands such as Green Day, Metallica, and Nirvana use these sounds in several songs. Palm muting is also common in folk music because it softens the chords, giving dynamic variety to the music.

SLAP STRUMMING

Slap strumming incorporates light slaps against the strings to add a percussive beat to your guitar music. It's a neat way to play both chords and rhythm.

Guitarists such as John Mayer, Ed Sheeran, and James Taylor slap strum to make their music more engaging.

HOW TO SLAP STRUM

Strum as you normally would, then slap the string lightly using the palm or fingers of your hand — whichever feels more natural for you. The slap should be sharp and short.

Adding slap strumming along with other techniques makes your music dynamic, especially during solos. Play a song that you like and you're familiar with. Try incorporating slaps to see if it adds interest to the song.

PLAYING WITH A BACKING TRACK

Once you've mastered your skills, you can move on to playing with a back track. If you've ever seen a guitarist play with a band, you'll notice them keeping time and blending with the other instruments. Practicing with back tracks will help improve your skills and give you the confidence to play with other people.

A back track is all about keeping rhythm. Rhythm is important for all genres and songs. It also makes you sound more professional and skilled, so it takes you from being a beginner to a more experienced player.

Backing tracks include drums, bass, and any other instrument you can imagine playing with. They can contain only one other instrument or even a full orchestra. Check online for backing tracks to practice with. Many are free, and they come in all genres. You can also pause and slow down the music as you need.

METRONOME PRACTICE

Metronomes are devices that produce a steady *click* at a specific tempo. The clicks are measured in beats per minute, or BPM. No matter how much experience you have as a guitarist, a metronome can help you sharpen your timing, improve accuracy, and help you play more consistently.

Genre	Common BPM Range	Example Songs
Ballads/Slow Songs	50–80 BPM	"Tears in Heaven" - Eric Clapton (77 BPM)
Blues (Slow)	60–90 BPM	"Red House" - Jimi Hendrix (65 BPM)
Blues (Medium)	90–110 BPM	"Sweet Home Chicago" - Robert Johnson (100 BPM)
Blues (Fast)	110–140 BPM	"Pride and Joy" - Stevie Ray Vaughan (127 BPM)
Rock (Slow, Classic Rock)	80–110 BPM	"Stairway to Heaven" - Led Zeppelin (82–102 BPM)
Rock (Mid-Tempo, Classic Rock)	110–140 BPM	"Sweet Child O' Mine" - Guns N' Roses (125 BPM)
Rock (Fast, Hard Rock)	140–180 BPM	"We're Not Gonna Take It" - Twisted Sister (150 BPM)
Pop	90–120 BPM	"All Star" - Smash Mouth (104 BPM), "Virtual Insanity" - Jamiroquai (92 BPM)
Funk	90–130 BPM	"Superstition" - Stevie

		Wonder (100 BPM)
Jazz (Swing/Traditional)	100–150 BPM	"Autumn Leaves" - Jazz Standard (120 BPM)
Jazz (Bebop/Fast Jazz)	160–250 BPM	"Salt Peanuts" - Dizzy Gillespie (230 BPM)
Country (Slow, Ballad Style)	70–100 BPM	"Tennessee Whiskey" - Chris Stapleton (80 BPM)
Country (Upbeat/Honky Tonk)	110–140 BPM	"Folsom Prison Blues" - Johnny Cash (118 BPM)
Metal (Groove Metal/Heavy)	100–140 BPM	"Enter Sandman" - Metallica (123 BPM)
Metal (Thrash/Fast)	160–220 BPM	"Master of Puppets" - Metallica (212 BPM)
Punk Rock	140–200 BPM	"Blitzkrieg Bop" - Ramones (180 BPM)
Reggae	60–90 BPM	"Three Little Birds" - Bob Marley (76 BPM)
Hip-Hop (Guitar Riffs in Beats)	75–110 BPM	"Still D.R.E." - Dr. Dre (93 BPM)
Latin/Bossa Nova	120–160 BPM	"Girl from Ipanema" - Antonio Carlos Jobim (140

		BPM)
Flamenco	120–200 BPM	"Entre Dos Aguas" - Paco de Lucía (170 BPM)

CHORD BASICS AND PLAYING STYLES

Chords are the foundation of music, the words that make up the story. A chord is three or more notes played together to produce a pleasant harmony. Each chord is named for its root note, which is often followed by the third and fifth notes of the scale. However, many chord names contain additional descriptions based on their characteristics.

Smoothly transitioning between chords can take a lot of practice. Plus, finishing a chord and moving to the next one needs to happen as quickly as possible to prevent disruptions in your music.

There are several different chords, including seventh chords, power chords, and diminished or augmented chords. The most important chords to learn, though, are major and minor chords.

MAJOR CHORDS

The first chords to learn are major chords. They're considered "happy" chords because of the bright sounds they make. Major chords consist of three chords that are called a *triad*.

A major chord has the first, third, and perfect fifth of each major scale. For example, E major includes E, $G\sharp$, and B. Meanwhile, G major includes the notes G, B, and D.

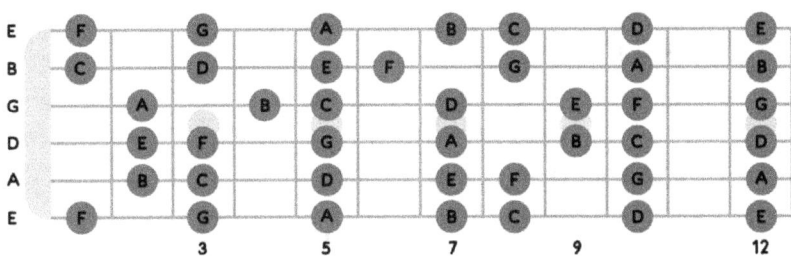

C MAJOR

This chord uses three fingers and is played using the top five strings. Keep in mind that guitar strings are numbered from bottom (thinnest) to top (thickest):

- Index finger on the first fret, second string (B)
- Middle finger on the second fret, fourth string (D)
- Ring finger on the third fret, fifth string (A)

Leave the other strings open and strum the top five strings. Apply enough pressure to the frets to hold the strings down, but don't strangle them.

G MAJOR

The G major chord also uses three fingers, but you'll strum all six strings:

- Index finger on the second fret, fifth string (*A*)
- Middle finger on the third fret, sixth string (*E*)
- Ring finger on the third fret, first string (*e*)

Strum all six strings.

A MAJOR

Like the C major chord, you'll only use five strings for this chord, but this time, you'll leave out the top string:

- Index finger on the second fret, fourth string (*D*)
- Middle finger on the second fret, third string (*G*)
- Ring finger on the second fret, second string (*B*)

Strum five strings down from *A* without playing the low *E* string.

D MAJOR

This chord uses only the bottom four strings:

- Index finger on the second fret, third string (*G*)
- Middle finger on the second fret, first string (*e*)
- Ring finger on the third fret, second string (*B*)

Strum the four thinnest strings and leave the rest alone.

E MAJOR

Use all six strings for this chord:

- Index finger on first fret, third string (*G*)
- Middle finger on second fret, fifth string (*A*)
- Ring finger on second fret, fourth string (*D*)

Strum all the strings.

Major Chords and Their Notes	
Chord	**Notes**
C major	C–E–G
C♯ (D♭) major	C♯–E♯ (F)–G♯

D major	D–F♯–A
D♯ (E♭) major	D♯–G–A♯ (E♭–G–Bb)
E major	E–G♯–B
F major	F–A–C
F♯ (G♭) major	F♯–A♯–C♯ (G♭–B♭–D♭)
G major	G–B–D
G♯ (A♭) major	G♯–C–D♯ (A♭–C–Eb)
A major	A–C♯–E
A♯ (B♭) major	A♯–D–F (B♭–D–F)
B major	B–D♯–F♯

MINOR CHORDS

Minor chords evoke feelings of sadness. They're used for moody music and include a root, a flattened third, and a fifth.

"Hurt" by Nine Inch Nails (subsequently covered by Johnny Cash) and "Losing My Religion" by R.E.M. both use minor keys to create their unique sounds. Minor chords are often denoted with a lowercase *m* or *min*.

A MINOR

This chord can be challenging for beginners, but it's good to learn once you've built up some dexterity. A minor uses the bottom five strings, leaving *E*, the thickest, out.

- Index finger on first fret, second string (*B*)
- Middle finger on second fret, fourth string (*D*)
- Ring finger on second fret, third string (*G*)

Strum all strings except for *E* (the thickest).

D MINOR

Considered by many to be the saddest of all chords, D minor uses only the bottom four strings:

- Index finger on the first fret, first string (*e*)
- Middle finger on second fret, third string (*G*)
- Ring finger on third fret, second string (*B*)

Strum from the fourth string (*D*) down.

BARRE CHORDS

Another common type of chord is the barre chord. When you play a barre chord, you'll have to push multiple strings with one finger, creating a bar across the strings. The B minor chord is one example.

B MINOR

- Index finger across the second fret, first-fifth strings
- Middle finger on the third fret, second string (*B*)
- Ring finger on the fourth fret, fifth string (*A*)
- Pinky on the fourth fret, fourth string (*D*)

POWER CHORDS

Some of the most iconic guitar music of all time uses power chords that are made up of two notes, traditionally the root and fifth. However, they're not technically chords because they lack a third note; in music theory, two simultaneous notes separated by an interval are called *dyads*.

Power chords are most commonly used on electric guitar, generally in rock. They're written as the letter of the note followed by the number 5.

A5

- Index finger on the fifth fret of the sixth string
- Middle finger on the seventh fret of the fifth string
- Ring finger on the seventh fret of the fourth string

Strum the top three (thickest) strings.

B5

- Index finger on the seventh fret of the sixth string
- Middle finger on the ninth fret of the fifth string
- Ring finger on the ninth fret of the fourth string

Strum the top three strings.

C5

- Index finger on the eighth fret of the sixth string
- Middle finger on the tenth fret of the fifth string
- Ring finger on the tenth fret of the fourth string

Strum the top three strings.

D5

- Index finger on the tenth fret of the sixth string
- Middle finger on the twelfth fret of the fifth string
- Ring finger on the twelfth fret of the fourth string

Strum the top three strings.

E5

- Index finger on the twelfth fret of the sixth string
- Middle finger on the fourteenth fret of the fifth string
- Ring finger on the fourteenth fret of the fourth string

Strum the top three strings.

F5

- Index finger on the first fret of the sixth string
- Middle finger on the third fret of the fifth string

- Ring finger on the third fret of the fourth string

Strum the top three strings.

G5

- Index finger on the third fret of the sixth string
- Middle finger on the fifth fret of the fifth string
- Ring finger on the fifth fret of the fourth string

Strum the top three strings.

OPEN CHORDS VS. CLOSED CHORDS

When you're learning to play, you'll reach a point where visualization is necessary. To fully understand chords, you'll need to know whether they're open or closed.

As their name suggests, open chords leave at least one string open, making them the easiest chords to play. C major and G major are two commonly used open chords.

Closed chords require all strings to be fretted. Barre chords are one type of closed chord, but the reverse is not always true. Think of it like geometry: All squares are rectangles, but not all rectangles are squares.

Unlike open chords, closed chords can be used anywhere on the neck, making them more versatile. However, closed chords require more experience and finger strength to accomplish.

Ultimately, each type of chord is used for different sounds. Open chords are great for folk, pop, and country, while closed chords are ideal for jazz and blues.

CHORD CHARTS

Once you're familiar with basic chords, you'll want to expand your musical arsenal by learning new ones. Chord charts provide a visual guide to learn finger placement and notes for every chord imaginable.

Chord charts are formed of a grid that depicts the fretboard. The vertical lines illustrate the six strings of the guitar, starting at the left with the sixth and thickest string, *E*, and ending on the right with the first string, *e*. Likewise, the horizontal lines represent frets, with the top row as the first fret. It might help to imagine the chart as an upright fretboard.

At the top of some charts, you'll find the letters *O* and *X*. The former, *O*, indicates that the string below it should be left open, while the latter, *X*, means that string should be muted or omitted when strumming.

Dots inside the grid indicate which fret to press on each string, provided it isn't open or muted. Some charts add numbers inside the dots to indicate which finger to use and a *T* to represent your thumb.

HOW TO READ A CHORD CHART

1. Start at the top of the chart, placing your fingers where the dots specify.

2. Check for Xs (muted strings), and make sure you leave them out when strumming.

3. Strum the chord slowly at first to be sure each note rings clearly.

4. Practice switching between chords to build finger strength, dexterity, and muscle memory.

Once you understand chord charts, you'll be able to learn and play just about any song. Keep your favorite charts handy and refer back to them as needed.

G Major

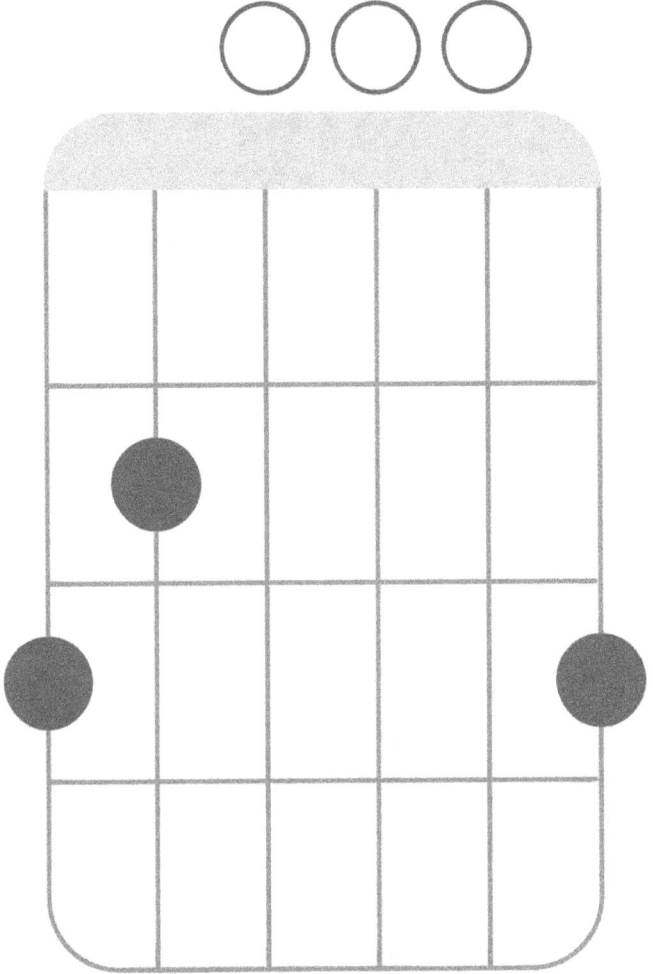

C Major

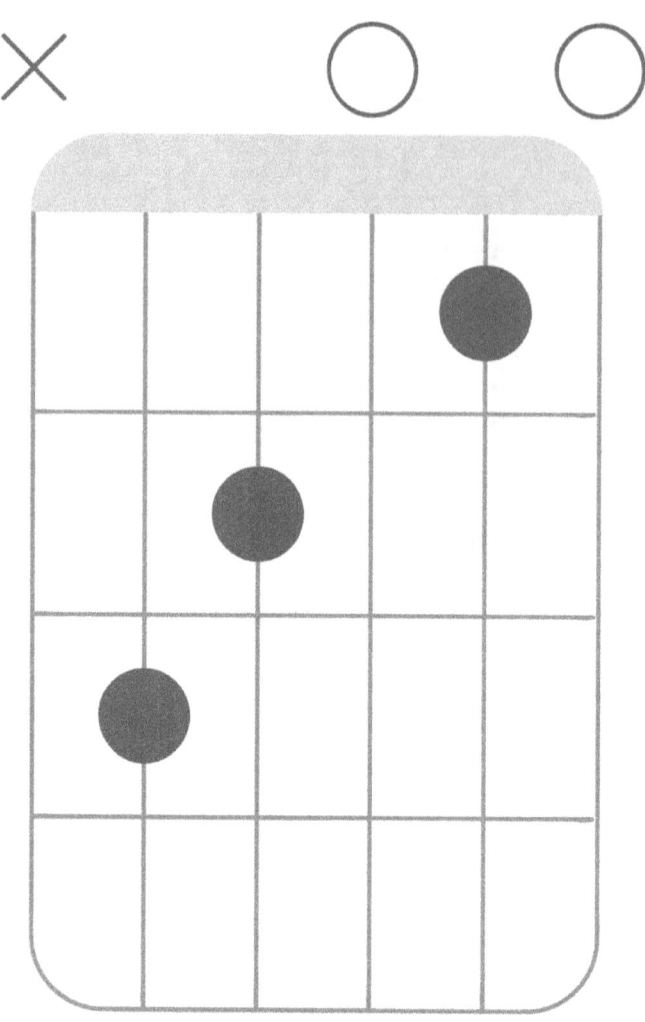

D Major

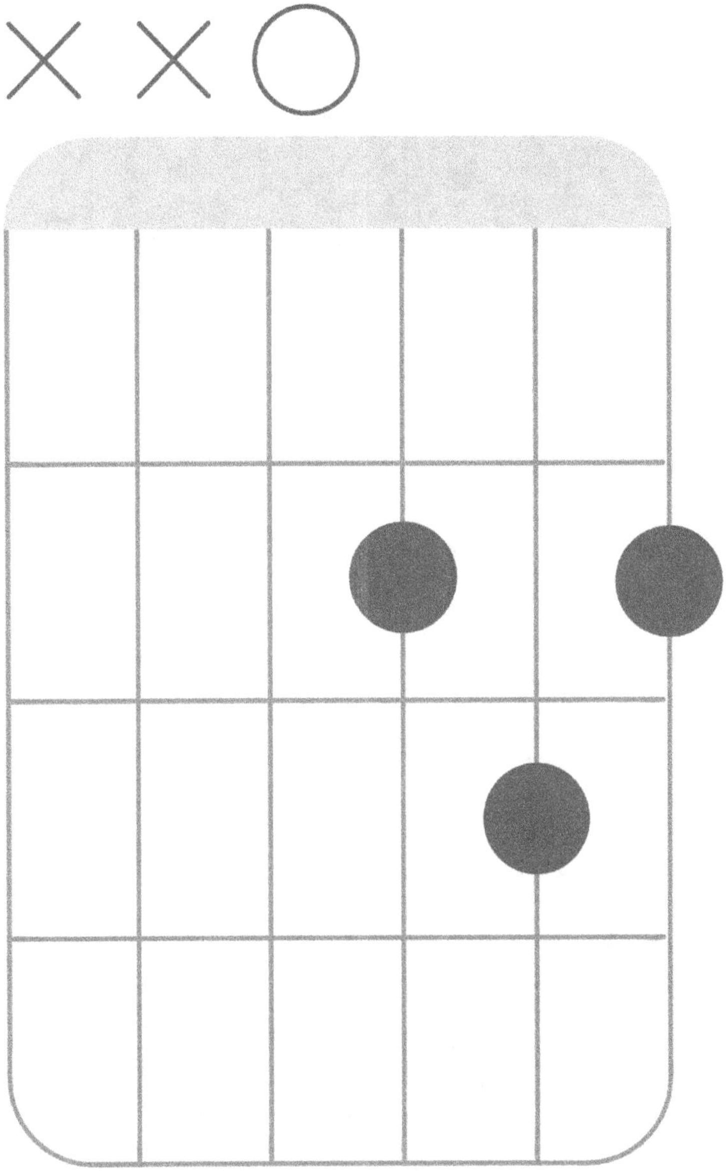

E Minor

DEVELOPING SMOOTH TRANSITIONS BETWEEN CHORDS

If you've ever listened to music, you've already heard chord progressions in action. You might not have known the term, but notes and chords can't become music without chord progressions.

Being comfortable with not only the chords but their progression is the key to mastering the guitar. Once you get the hang of a few common progressions, you'll be able to play limitless songs and even create your own music.

WHAT IS A CHORD PROGRESSION?

A chord progression is a series of chords played in sequence to create musical structure and harmony. Think of chord progression as the foundation that melodies are built on.

Various progressions evoke different moods, and while some are simple, others are complex and take time to master. Progressions may sound like they could continue forever with no end or resolve in a satisfying conclusion.

COMMON CHORD PROGRESSIONS

Certain chord progressions appear in thousands of songs, and these are a great place to start. Due to their widespread popularity, being familiar with their structure will save you time when learning new songs.

THE I–V–vi–IV (1–5–6–4) PROGRESSION

One of the most famous chord progressions in popular music, the I–V–vi–IV progression can be found in "Let it Be" (the Beatles), "With or Without You" (U2), and "Someone Like You" (Adele).

In the key of C major, the chord progression would be as follows:

C major (I)

G major (V)

A minor (vi)

F major (IV)

Using this progression produces a smooth but satisfying sound.

THE 12-BAR BLUES PROGRESSION

If you've ever listened to rock, blues, or jazz, you've probably heard the 12-bar blues progression. Also known as "blues changes," the 12-bar is a repeating pattern of three chords. For example, in E major, it would be E major, A major, and B major.

SMOOTH TRANSITIONS

Moving smoothly between chords is one of the harder skills for a guitarist to master. Transitioning from one chord to the next can feel awkward and clunky at first, but with practice, you'll get the hang of it.

Music is all about rhythm and flow, so you want to avoid taking too long between chords and breaking up the song. Gaps in the music can cause the song to lose momentum.

MOVING AND PLACING YOUR FINGERS CORRECTLY

Correct finger placement is vital when transitioning between chords. Many beginners make the mistake of completely lifting their hand off the fretboard, which wastes time and makes transitioning much harder. Minimizing movement keeps your fingers close to the fretboard.

Lift your fingers only as much as needed to move from string to string. Try working through the movements in slow motion until you're comfortable, then speed up until you reach the correct tempo.

Visualizing your next move can help you become more familiar as you build your skill. Mental preparation will build instinctive movement. While you might have to start with moving your fingers one at a time, as you gain more experience, you should be able to move all your fingers at once. This will speed up your chord changes to avoid breaks in your music.

FINGER ANCHORS AND HOW THEY HELP YOU

Finger anchors are a key way to promote smooth chord transitions. When you're changing chords, you can sometimes keep one finger on the same string, making it easier to move the others. Here are some examples:

- **G major to D major:** Keep your ring finger on the third fret of the B string when you change.
- **C major to A minor:** Keep your index and middle fingers in the same place, moving only your ring finger.

EXERCISES

Let's review some good exercises to improve your skills.

ONE-MINUTE DRILL

Pick two chords and set a timer for one minute. See how many times you can change between the two chords in that minute. You want to get fast enough to change 60 times or more per minute.

Once you've mastered those two chords, choose another two and continue to work your way through them.

30-SECOND COUNTDOWN

Once you feel like you've mastered the first exercise, try this one. Set a timer for 30 seconds and choose three to five chords. Practice getting through all of them, and see how many times you can go through them in 30 seconds.

STRUMMING TECHNIQUES FOR RHYTHM

When you watch someone playing guitar, you see their hand moving up and down gently across the strings. This strumming motion creates rhythm, which is the force that keeps the song moving. Strumming isn't just about randomly hitting strings; it's how you control the sound, create musical textures, and generate the energy for the song.

When strumming, using a combination of different strumming techniques gives your music depth. Downstrokes, upstrokes, and strumming patterns are what make guitar music so interesting.

CHAPTER FIVE:
THE HISTORY AND LEGACY
OF THE GUITAR

HISTORY OF
THE GUITAR

ANCIENT ORIGINS

Dating back to 3,000 BCE, stringed instruments have long been an important part of culture and society. Music has always appealed to humans, and our ancestors were no exception. The vibrating strings that captivated ancient civilizations are remarkably similar to the stringed instruments that delight us today.

THE EARLIEST STRINGED INSTRUMENTS

The oldest surviving string instruments are known as the Lyres of Ur. These four instruments date back to around 2,500 BCE. The amazing lyres were found in modern-day Iraq, an area that was once ancient Mesopotamia. Discovered in the Royal Cemetery of Ur, they belonged to a family of instruments called *plucked chordophones*, which simply means their strings are designed to be plucked.

The Lyres of Ur were intricately decorated with precious metals and gems, demonstrating their importance in religious and royal ceremonies. Lyres are considered one of the earliest direct ancestors of the guitar. They were used throughout Egypt, Greece, and other Mediterranean cultures.

Some other early string instruments include the harp, lute, ravanastron, and the se, all of which contributed to the rise of the modern guitar.

- **Harp:** Not specifically linked to any one culture, the harp dates back over 4,000 years. Its strings stretch along a curved frame and create music when plucked.
- **Ravanastron:** Originating in India, this bowed string instrument was made from a hollow cylindrical body with strings of gut or silk.
- **Se:** This Chinese instrument from 1100 BCE featured movable bridges and silk strings.

Other instruments also played a significant role in ancient music. Drums and percussion instruments have been discovered at archaeological sites dating back 24,000 years. Some of these drums were made from mammoth bones and reindeer antlers.

Wind instruments also have a long history. The earliest flutes date back approximately 40,000 years. Specifically, flutes made of bird bones and mammoth ivory have been carbon dated back to 36,000 years ago, which means people have been playing instruments longer than they've been using the wheel.

ANCIENT GREECE'S INFLUENCE ON THE GUITAR

Ancient Greece used many instruments we're familiar with thanks to art and records kept by famous poets, historians, and inventors of the time. Their love of the arts and music, which they incorporated into their daily life, led to many advancements in their instruments.

One unique instrument they were fond of was the kithara, which was a "professional" version of the lyre. The design incorporated a wooden sound box at the base that worked as a resonator. It was played by skilled musicians, including those performing in royal courts, religious ceremonies, and public competitions.

Greek mythology is riddled with tales of gods and heroes playing instruments, which is just further proof that music was crucial to the ancient Greeks' everyday life.

MEDIEVAL GROWTH AND THE SPREAD OF INSTRUMENTS

During the medieval era, many new stringed instruments evolved or were introduced to Europe through cultural exchange. It wasn't until 1,000 years after the fall of the Roman Empire that people began to show a keen interest in Greek and Roman texts. This rediscovery of ancient art and literature led to a deeper appreciation of music and an explosion of ideas.

The Renaissance further facilitated the spread and refinement of musical instruments as global trade increased. The oud was brought to Europe by Moors from the Middle East and parts of Africa. With a pear-shaped body, short neck, and no frets, it was well suited for complex melodies and improvisation. The oud was immensely popular in Islamic culture, and later influenced the development of European stringed instruments.

The lute was developed from the oud in an attempt to adapt the instrument to Western music. The lute was a fretted string instrument with a rounded back that's closely associated with medieval and Renaissance music. It's also one of the most frequently depicted instruments in Renaissance artwork.

SPAIN'S CONTRIBUTION TO THE GUITAR'S EVOLUTION

While the lute became dominant in much of Europe, Spain developed its own unique instrument: the vihuela. With a flat back and curved body, it closely resembled today's modern guitar. Musicians often used a combination of plucking, bowing, and strumming with the vihuela.

Unlike the lute, some variations of the vihuela featured paired courses of strings, similar to a modern 12-string guitar. It was particularly popular in Spanish courts, where musicians both plucked and strummed to create rhythmic and melodic textures.

In the seventeenth and eighteenth centuries, the vihuela's popularity gradually declined in favor of the five-stringed baroque guitar. In the nineteenth century, a sixth string was added, and six-string guitars became popular with aristocrats.

By the end of the sixteenth century, the guitar-like shape of the vihuela and baroque guitar had become standard, setting the stage for further refinements in the Renaissance and beyond. While electric and steel-string acoustic guitars were still centuries away, the craftsmen and musicians who shaped music across the ancient world laid the foundation for these modern-day instruments.

HOW THE GUITAR
BECAME FAMOUS

At the beginning of the twentieth century, the guitar was considered more of a regional, folksy instrument rather than the recognizable instrument it is today. The guitar's amazing rise to fame has been shaped by many different genres and cultural shifts. The guitar played a massive role in folk, blues, and early music. It also gained popularity during the jazz and big band era and became a defining element of the folk revival and rock explosion from the 1950s to the 1970s.

FOLK, BLUES, AND EARLY POPULAR MUSIC

Before recorded music, the guitar was primarily used in folk traditions due to its portability and versatility. The guitar's affordability and compatibility with vocals made it a folk musician's mainstay.

In the eighteenth and nineteenth centuries, European settlers brought guitars to the Americas, where they were quickly incorporated into rural folk traditions. Guitars were used to accompany storytelling ballads and local protest songs.

Going into the late nineteenth century, the guitar became a staple of blues music, particularly in the South. Blues guitarists mastered fingerpicking and the bottleneck slide technique that characterized the genre's unique sound. The bottleneck slide technique involves using a smooth object—like the neck of a glass bottle—to slide along the strings of the guitar.

Famous blues guitarists such as Robert Johnson, Charley Patton, and Son House reimagined the guitar, defining it as a lead instrument. The 12-bar blues chord progression originated during this period, eventually becoming one of the most important frameworks for modern music.

During the early twentieth century, the guitar started to appear in popular music recordings. Variations of ragtime, vaudeville, and country musicians used guitars to provide rhythm, and as recording became more popular, so did the guitar. Radio and phonographs made music a mainstay in the home. Well-known artists such as Jimmie Rodgers and the Carter Family solidified the guitar in country music.

GUITAR IN JAZZ AND BIG BAND

As guitars gained momentum in country, jazz musicians began to experiment with guitars as well. In the 1920s and 1930s, jazz was the most popular music genre in the U.S., and the guitar was becoming a key element.

Guitars started out as rhythm instruments in jazz bands, reinforcing chord changes and harmonies alongside banjos and pianos. However, as musical tastes changed, guitarists needed a louder, more prominent sound.

During this period, the electric guitar made its debut, allowing guitarists to pump up the volume. While guitarists originally tried to avoid distortion, artists like Jimi Hendrix and The Kings leaned into the gritty sound to create unique music.

The Gibson ES-150, one of the first commercially successful electric guitars, hit the market in 1936. Jazz guitarist Charlie Christian, guitarist for the Benny Goodman Sextet, became one of the first musicians to use the electric guitar for melodic improvisation. This established the guitar as a possible lead voice for jazz, paving the way for Django Reinhardt, Wes Montgomery, and Joe Pass.

The 1930s and 1940s became the big band era, characterized by swing music and large jazz orchestras that typically included saxophones, trumpets, trombones, and rhythm sections. Big band music rose to prominence in Chicago and New York. It evolved from early jazz traditions but really took off during World War II over the airwaves.

Guitarists such as Freddie Green of the Count Basie Orchestra refined swing rhythm guitar, using four-to-the-bar strumming to drive large ensembles. Although guitar still competed with horns, pianos, and drums, its use in jazz continued to rise. This period set the stage for future genres where the guitar would take center stage.

FOLK REVIVAL AND ROCK EXPLOSION

By the 1950s, the guitar was not just an accompaniment instrument but was rapidly becoming the symbol of modern music. Folk music was revived by artists like Woody Guthrie, Pete Seeger, Bob Dylan, and Joan Baez, who emphasized the use of acoustic guitar for protest songs, storytelling, and political commentary.

Songs like Bob Dylan's "Blowin' in the Wind" and Pete Seeger's "We Shall Overcome" demonstrated the guitar's ability to carry a simple and powerful message, a trait that appealed to youth and activists. Around the same time, rock and roll was born, solidifying the guitar's place in popular music.

Early rock pioneers such as Chuck Berry, Buddy Holly, and Elvis Presley used the electric guitar's newfound amplification to create energetic, rhythm-driven songs that especially resonated with young audiences. Buddy Holly, with his Fender Stratocaster, became an icon of the genre.

Improvements to electric guitars and amplification during the 1960s and 1970s caused an explosion of rock music. The rise of distortion, feedback, and effects pedals allowed musicians to push the instrument's boundaries.

Many iconic bands like the Beatles, the Rolling Stones, Led Zeppelin, and the Jimi Hendrix Experience transformed rock into a culture-defining force. Hendrix made huge strides in revolutionizing guitar playing by mastering feedback, wah pedals, and overdriven amplifiers.

Multiple subgenres of rock have emerged, including hard rock, progressive rock, punk, and heavy metal, all of which place the electric guitar at the forefront. Guitar heroes like Eric Clapton, Jimmy Page, Eddie Van Halen, and David Gilmour stretched the guitar's possibilities, and punk bands like the Ramones and Sex Pistols embraced the guitar for its raw power.

THE EVOLUTION OF
THE ELECTRIC GUITAR

The electric guitar traces its roots back to the early twentieth century when musicians and engineers sought ways to amplify the sound of traditional acoustic guitars. Before amplification, guitarists in jazz and big band settings struggled to be heard over brass and percussion instruments. It doesn't matter how talented a guitarist is if no one can hear them play.

The need for greater volume and sustain led to the development of electric amplification and, eventually, the electric guitar. The first commercially successful electric guitar was the Rickenbacker Electro A-22, nicknamed the "Frying Pan." It was developed in 1931 by George Beauchamp and Paul Barth.

The Frying Pan was a lap steel guitar with a pair of horseshoe magnets serving as the pickup, but it needed an external amplifier. By the 1940s, the desire for louder, feedback-resistant guitars led to the design of solid-body guitars that produced less feedback at high volumes.

In 1950, Leo Fender released the Broadcaster, which was later renamed the Telecaster. It was the first commercially successful solid-body electric guitar. It wasn't much later that Gibson released the Les Paul model in 1952, proving that the electric guitar was here to stay.

DEFINING GUITAR PERFORMANCES

Live guitar music has gone through a fascinating journey, with experimentation and artistic expression unlocking more than was ever thought possible on the guitar. The transition from the early days of live performance to the complex techniques employed by famous guitarists today reflects changes in musical tastes, technological advancements, and shifting cultural influences.

Over decades, the guitar has evolved not only as an instrument but also as a way to communicate with audiences. During this shift, certain performances stand out, showcasing the guitar in ways like never before. In rare instances, guitar solos have rocked the world and changed perceptions of what the guitar is capable of.

JIMI HENDRIX AT WOODSTOCK (1969)

Held August 15–18, 1969, on a dairy farm in Bethel, New York, Woodstock is considered a defining moment in the 1960s counterculture movement. The festival focused on "peace and love" and featured some of the most famous musicians of that time.

One of those artists was Jimi Hendrix, and his performance remains an iconic moment in rock history. His rendition of "The Star-Spangled Banner" was one of the most memorable performances of the festival.

Hendrix was the highest-paid performer at Woodstock and closed the festival. However, due to severe delays, he didn't perform until the morning of Monday, August 18, 1969. He played for a diminished crowd of about 30,000 people, down from the original audience of nearly 400,000.

Although the crowd was smaller, Hendrix's unique interpretation of the song made a raw, emotional statement that transfixed his audience. Using distortion, feedback, and a wah pedal, he transformed the song into a symbol of political turbulence. This performance was both celebrated and controversial at the time.

Hendrix broke ground in the manipulation of the electric guitar because of his skill at string bending, fingerpicking, and using feedback. Much of his audience at Woodstock had never heard anything like the sounds Hendrix produced, and the performance left them inspired and uplifted. The music also synced with the spirit of defiance displayed in their call for peace.

ERIC CLAPTON'S *UNPLUGGED* (1992)

Another transformative performance in guitar history is Eric Clapton's 1992 *Unplugged* concert. Already well known as an electric guitarist, he set himself apart as an acoustic guitarist when his MTV special showcased another side of his artistry.

MTV's *Unplugged* concert series was designed to showcase artists in an intimate, stripped-down environment, and Clapton's 1992 performance became one of its most famous episodes. The intimate setting of this performance was very different from Clapton's typical spectacles. The small venue gave audiences a chance to hear Clapton play in the truest form without any electrical enhancements or distractions.

The resulting album went on to win six Grammy Awards, including Album of the Year and Best Rock Song for his acoustic rework of "Layla." The original version of "Layla," released in 1970 with Derek and the Dominos, was an electrified, high-energy rock anthem. It was written about Clapton's unrequited love for Pattie Boyd, then married to George Harrison. The vulnerability and emotional depth of the subject matter shone in his soulful fingerpicking and heartfelt delivery, giving the song new power and dimension.

Unplugged spoke to both long-term fans and new listeners alike. The concert followed the tragic death of Clapton's four-year-old son, Conor, in March 1991. This grief shaped the raw emotional force of the performance, especially with the song "Tears in Heaven," which Clapton wrote for his late son. It remains one of the best-selling live albums of all time, with over 26 million copies sold worldwide.

EDDIE VAN HALEN'S "ERUPTION" (LATE 1970s– EARLY 1980s)

Van Halen's performance of "Eruption" is hands down one of the most influential moments in guitar history. Originally performed live in the late 1970s and early 1980s, this guitar solo quickly became the centerpiece of the band's performances. "Eruption" was officially recorded and included on Van Halen's 1978 self-titled debut album.

Van Halen combined intricate finger-tapping, lightning-fast legato runs, and harmonic tricks that had never been heard in rock music.

The solo was a revolutionary reimagining of what the guitar could do.

Van Halen wasn't the first to use finger-tapping techniques, which were relatively common in jazz and classical music. However, Eddie Van Halen revolutionized the method with unparalleled speed, precision, and showmanship. His two-handed tapping and use of the whammy bar set a new standard for rock guitarists.

What truly set Van Halen apart was an amazing balance of mind-blowing technicality and raw emotion. His solo wasn't just a series of notes but a whole story with a sense of urgency and passion that resonated with audiences. It became clear that guitar solos could be more than just a showcase of skill; they could also be an integral part of a song, carrying emotional weight and providing a focal point in live performances.

B. B. KING AT THE FILLMORE (1969)

Live guitar performance reached another landmark moment with legendary blues guitarist B. B. King's performance at the Fillmore in 1969. King was known for his unique, expressive style, and the Fillmore show demonstrated exactly how deeply he could connect with audiences.

King's signature technique was using his fingers to bend the string on his guitar, lovingly named Lucille. His Fillmore performance was a legendary example of how he could mix blues, jazz, and gospel into a single, soulful sound unlike anything else.

"The Thrill is Gone" is a prime example of how King's playing evoked deep emotion from his listeners. The combination of powerful vocals and masterful use of vibrato captivated audiences, establishing this as a performance to remember.

JIMMY PAGE IN *THE SONG REMAINS THE SAME* (1973)

One of the most iconic live guitar moments from the 1970s is Jimmy Page's performance in Led Zeppelin's concert film *The Song Remains the Same* (1976), which captured the band at Madison Square Garden in 1973. Page's playing, often described as a combination of precise technique and raw power, is at its most captivating during the footage of "Stairway to Heaven."

This performance marked the ultimate moment for Page's improvisational skills and technical ability to shine. Filled with soaring bends, lightning-fast runs, and an amazing use of dynamic shifts, Page's epic guitar solo took the audience on a musical journey.

Page was set apart, not only by his technical proficiency but also by his ability to form an emotional connection with the audience. He created a visceral experience that reflected the true spirit of the song.

CLASSICAL MUSIC AND THE GUITAR

Classical guitar has helped shape the landscape of music with an expressive sound that complements classical compositions. Unlike the steel strings used in folk and rock music, classical guitar is characterized by nylon strings. Warm tones and intricate fingerpicking define this genre.

While many classical guitarists have taken the instrument and created beautiful music, some stand out as legendary examples.

ANDRÉS SEGOVIA (1983–1987)

Spanish musician Andrés Segovia is credited with elevating the guitar into a legitimate concert instrument. Before Segovia, guitars were dismissed by many as instruments solely for folksy or blues music.

Segovia commissioned and inspired works from well-known composers of his time, including Manuel Ponce, Joaquín Rodrigo, Heitor Villa-Lobos, and Federico Moreno Torroba. He also transcribed pieces from Bach, Albéniz, and Granados, broadening what was available for classical guitarists at the time.

While making music more widely available, he also developed a new technique that involved precise right-hand movements focusing on tonal control, clarity, and dynamics. His unique approach to fingering and hand positioning would become the standard for classical guitar.

Since Segovia recorded extensively throughout his life, he left behind an invaluable collection of performances. His influence affected generations of guitarists, including notable musicians such as John Williams, Julian Bream, and Christopher Parkening.

Segovia received numerous honors, including a Grammy Lifetime Achievement Award and a knighthood from Spain, guaranteeing his place in musical history.

JOHN WILLIAMS (b. 1941)

John Williams is an Australian guitarist famous for ensemble playing and his ability to bring modern classical guitar to a broad audience. He is well known for flawless precision and effortless execution. His command of technique allows him to play with unreal control, which has helped set the standard for classical guitarists.

Like Segovia, Williams has played a huge role in expanding classical guitar repertoire. While he has performed and recorded works by composers such as Joaquín Rodrigo, Heitor Villa-Lobos, Agustín Barrios, and Leo Brouwer, he's also known for exploring jazz, folk, and world music.

Williams's recording of Rodrigo's "Concierto de Aranjuez" is one of the most famous interpretations of the piece. Williams studied at the Royal College of Music in London under Segovia's influence but developed his own unique style. This has led to differences in opinion regarding Segovia's traditionalist views and Williams's more modern approach to classical music.

Having received numerous awards and honors for his contributions to music, Williams remains an iconic figure in the world of classical guitar.

FINGERPICKING AND CLASSICAL GUITAR TECHNIQUES

Classical guitar is known for its unique fingerpicking style, which differentiates it from other genres. Instead of using a pick, classical guitarists pluck the strings with fingers and fingernails. This grants more control over the sound, making it easier to vary volume, tone, and expression. The dominant hand's fingers each move on their own to create smooth, flowing melodies.

Here are some important classical guitar techniques:

- **Apoyando (rest stroke):** This is when a guitarist plucks a string, then lets their finger rest on the next string to make the sound stronger and fuller.
- **Tirando (free stroke):** With this technique, the finger doesn't rest on the next string after plucking, which creates a lighter and smoother sound.
- **Tremolo:** This involves quickly repeating a note with multiple fingers to create a continuous, shimmering sound.
- **Rasgueado:** This technique derives from flamenco music. It involves strumming with the fingers spaced apart to sound each note multiple times in quick succession.

- **Harmonics:** By lightly touching the string in certain spots while plucking, guitarists can produce soft, bell-like tones.

These techniques are what make classical guitar playing so expressive and unique, drawing in audiences and compelling them to love the guitar.

FAMOUS CLASSICAL GUITAR PIECES

While there are many amazing classical pieces out there, a few stand out for their melodies, the emotions they evoke, and the level of technical skill they demand.

"CONCIERTO DE ARANJUEZ" (JOAQUÍN RODRIGO)

This is considered a classical guitar masterpiece because of its beautiful, evocative melodies and integration of Spanish folk elements. It's inspired by the serene beauty of the Royal Palace of Aranjuez gardens in Spain and creates a sense of tranquility for the audience by portraying the natural imagery and peace of the gardens. This piece also demands a high level of technical skills from the guitarist.

"RECUERDOS DE LA ALHAMBRA" (FRANCISCO TÀRREGA"

With a mesmerizing tremolo technique and profound emotional depth, this challenging piece creates the illusion of sustained notes.

The tremolo technique captures the sound of fountains within the Alhambra, a palace in Granada, Spain. This piece has been performed by some of the greatest guitarists in history.

"ASTURIAS" (ISAAC ALBÉNIZ)

Originally composed for piano, this piece has become a standard for classical guitar due to its intricate melodies and dramatic dynamic shifts. The technical demands of the piece showcase the guitar's amazing abilities.

"Asturias" captures the rhythmic and melodic elements of flamenco with driving cadences and sudden dynamic changes. It's one of the most well-known and frequently performed classical guitar pieces. Many consider it a staple of any guitarist's repertoire.

"CHACONNE FROM PARTITA NO. 2 IN D MINOR" (J.S. BACH, ARR. SEGOVIA)

A great classical piece with musical depth and complex variations, the repeating themes of this piece form a tapestry of musical ideas. The tone is often interpreted as a lament, possibly over the death of Bach's first wife, making it a deeply moving piece for audiences.

Like many of Bach's compositions, it's challenging for guitarists. The piece includes complex fingerings, intricate rhythms, and a wide range of dynamics, making it a piece that showcases virtuosity.

CHAPTER SIX:
EXPLORING BLUES
AND JAZZ STYLES

Each genre of music has its own unique take on guitar. Learning how different genres create music their own is part of becoming an expert guitarist. After all, knowing the history of your favorite style of music can make you appreciate it even more.

JAZZ MUSIC AND THE GUITAR

The guitar has played a critical role in the evolution of jazz, developing alongside the early roots of the New Orleans modern-day jazz fusion. Unlike the classical guitar, jazz traditionally uses steel strings and picks, though fingerstyle playing isn't unheard of. The smooth, complex sounds that characterize this genre create a harmonic, rhythmic sound. From swing to bebop and contemporary jazz, guitar has been essential in shaping the sound of jazz.

EARLY JAZZ

In the 1910s and 1920s, guitar was used for rhythm in jazz, either playing along with or replacing a banjo. The early days of jazz were known as "Dixieland jazz" or "New Orleans jazz," with small ensembles that focused on improvisation. The guitar played a steady accompaniment to maintain tempo.

NOTABLE JAZZ PLAYERS OF THE TIME

EDDIE LANG (1902–1933): THE FATHER OF JAZZ GUITAR

Born in Philadelphia, Pennsylvania, as Salvatore Massaro, Eddie Lang was one of the first guitarists to elevate the guitar in jazz music, giving it a prominent voice as a solo instrument. Although he started out playing violin, Lang switched to the banjo in his late teens, then settled on guitar a few years later. In the early 1920s, he played with dance bands and small jazz groups, which allowed him to develop the reputation of a gifted accompanist.

His career really took off when he started playing with cornetist Bix Beiderbecke and violinist Joe Venuti. Lang and Venuti developed a groundbreaking guitar-violin duo, blending jazz with classical influences and laying the foundation for future jazz guitarists.

In the late 1920s, Lang joined Paul Whiteman's orchestra, a popular dance band of the time. As Whiteman sought to merge jazz with symphonic arrangements, Lang's guitar helped bridge the gap between classical sophistication and jazz improvisation. While he was a skilled rhythm accompanist, his real genius lay in melodic single-note solos, which wasn't common for guitarists of the era.

Sadly, Lang's career was cut short in 1933 when he died at the age of 30 after what should have been a routine tonsillectomy. Despite his short life, Lang's influence on jazz guitar was profound. His innovations laid the groundwork for jazz legends like Django Reinhardt and Charlie Christian.

FREDDIE GREEN (1911–1987): MR. RHYTHM

A huge influence for the swing era and a core member of the Count Basie Orchestra for 50 years, Green perfected the art of comping. This technique involves playing steady, four-to-the-bar chordal rhythms to provide the essential pulse of the big band sound.

Born in Charleston, South Carolina, Green lived a life full of music. He began with the banjo as a child, then switched to the guitar as jazz gained popularity. Moving to New York City opened him up to a world of opportunities, and he established himself as a reliable and swinging rhythm guitarist. He eventually earned the nickname "Mr. Rhythm."

In 1937, Count Basie heard Green play at a Harlem club and was so impressed that he offered Green a spot in his band. This marked the beginning of a lifelong partnership that would define big band rhythm guitar.

Green's work can be heard on classic albums such as *One O'Clock Jump* and *April in Paris*. Although jazz evolved in the 1950s and 1960s, Green remained committed to his style, and his legacy proves that great rhythm guitar is just as valuable as soloing.

JAZZ IN THE
1930s AND 1940s

The advent of the electric guitar revolutionized jazz. Suddenly, electric guitars could compete in volume with other instruments like horns and pianos. Thus, guitar solos gained popularity in the genre. During this time, advancements helped set a new tone, and certain guitarists really stood out.

CHARLIE CHRISTIAN (1916–1942)

Among the first electric guitarists, Charlie Christian was instrumental in redefining the guitar's role in swing music as a viable lead instrument.

Born in Bonham, Texas, in 1916, Christian grew up in a musical household. His father, a blind musician, played the trumpet and guitar and passed his passion down to his sons. Like his brothers, Charlie became a musician, initially playing in a traditional rhythmic style to accompany blues and swing bands.

Even as a teenager, Christian stood out due to his ability to play single-note melodic lines, a technique uncommon for guitarists at the time. He drew inspiration from jazz horn players rather than fellow guitarists, mimicking the fluid phrasing of saxophonists and trumpeters. By the early 1930s, he'd already built a reputation in Oklahoma City, performing in jazz clubs and impressing audiences with his improvisational skills.

Christian's big break came in 1939 when renowned music producer John Hammond heard about Christian's talent.

Hammond arranged an audition with Benny Goodman, one of the most famous band leaders of the time.

In Goodman's band, Christian revolutionized swing guitar, using amplification to make the guitar a prominent solo instrument. His recordings with Goodman — including "Seven Come Eleven," "Airmail Special," and "Flying Home" — showcase his incredible melodic phrasing and improvisational fluidity.

While Christian gained fame in swing, he was also a key figure in the birth of bebop, a fast, harmonically complex style of jazz that emerged in the early 1940s. He spent much of his free time at Minton's Playhouse, a legendary Harlem jazz club, where he jammed with Thelonious Monk, Dizzy Gillespie, and Kenny Clarke.

It was there that Christian experimented with faster tempos, intricate melodic lines, and complex harmonies, all of which became defining features of bebop. His horn-like phrasing and ability to navigate rapid chord changes made him one of the first guitarists of true bebop style. His informal recordings at Minton's, such as "Swing to Bop," foreshadowed the future of jazz guitar.

Sadly, Christian's life was cut short when he succumbed to tuberculosis in 1942 at just 25 years old. Despite his brief career, his impact on jazz guitar was immense. He bridged the gap between swing and modern jazz, ensuring that the electric guitar would remain a central voice in jazz.

JAZZ OF THE
1940s AND 1950s

In the 1940s, bebop hit the scene. Guitarists learned to keep up with the speed and intensity of bebop with new techniques like single-note lines influenced by saxophonists and trumpeters. As their chords became more sophisticated, extended harmonies and special tones became more prominent.

TAL FARLOW (1921–1998)

Farlow was an innovative jazz guitarist who was well known for his bebop-era contributions. His nickname, "Octopus," came from his large hands and extraordinary reach across the fretboard. His unique style blended unorthodox playing with popular bebop music, making him one of the most exciting guitarists of his time.

Born in 1921 in Greensboro, North Carolina, Tal Farlow didn't initially pursue music, unlike most of his contemporaries. He worked as a sign painter for much of his early life and developed guitar skills as a hobby when he was 22. He was largely self-taught and, because of this, developed a distinctive style that set him apart from other guitarists of his time.

Despite being self-taught, Farlow was nonetheless inspired by jazz legends like Charlie Christian and Django Reinhardt, so he worked to master the skills they had. In the late 1940s, Farlow joined vibraphonist Red Norvo's trio and began to draw attention. The trio featured bassist Charles Mingus but lacked a drummer. The resulting groundbreaking instrumentation relied on the rhythmic interplay between guitar, bass, and vibraphone. Farlow's rapid single-note runs drove the group's sound.

As Farlow's popularity grew, he began recording albums under his own name and established himself as a premier bebop guitarist. His playing style was characterized by lightning-fast improvisation, intricate chord melodies, and an ability to shift seamlessly between rhythm and lead.

What made Farlow truly special was his ability to balance speed with musicality. While many guitarists prioritize technical showmanship, Farlow never lost sight of melody and harmonic depth.

Surprisingly, at the height of his career, Farlow stepped away from full-time music and returned to sign painting following his marriage in 1958. It seems that the backstage aspects of jazz weren't as appealing to Farlow as the music.

However, he continued to play and record sporadically, making a celebrated return in the 1970s and 1980s with albums such as *Guitar Player* and *Cookin' on All Burners*. Throughout his lifetime, he recorded over 26 albums. In 1962, Gibson released the Tal Farlow model guitar, and a documentary about him was released in 1981. He made such a big impact that a DVD was released in 2005, seven years after his death.

JAZZ OF THE
1950s AND 1960s

Hard bop evolved out of bebop, infusing jazz with blues, gospel, and R&B to create a soulful, grounded sound. Featuring driving rhythms with heavy backbeats, hard bop focused on a return to simpler melodies.

Around the same time, cool jazz, which had slowly gained popularity over the last couple of decades, was growing in direct opposition to the intensity of bebop. Favoring smoother tones, slower tempos, and relaxed improvisation, cool jazz often creates an introspective or atmospheric mood.

This period also saw the rise of modal jazz, which sought to break away from rapid chord changes and focus more on melodic improvisation within extended modal structures.

WES MONTGOMERY (1923–1968)

Born in Indianapolis, Indiana, in 1923, Montgomery grew up in a musical family but had no formal training. It wasn't until he heard a recording of Charlie Christian that he became captivated by the guitar. Determined to teach himself, he saved up to buy a guitar just so that he could transcribe Christian's solos note for note.

Despite his newfound passion for the guitar, Montgomery had a family to support, which meant he couldn't dedicate much time to music. During the day, he spent long hours working as a welder, and at night, he played at small clubs wherever he could get a gig.

He practiced quietly at home, which led to a unique thumb-picking technique that produced a warm, mellow tone. This technique might have been used to avoid disturbing his family.

Montgomery's early career saw him playing with his brothers, Monk and Buddy, in a band called The Mastersounds. However, it wasn't until he was discovered by Cannonball Adderley in 1959 that his career really took off.

Montgomery's approach to guitar technique was revolutionary. He popularized playing the same note on two different strings, an approach that became his signature. Adderley was so impressed that he convinced Riverside Records to sign Montgomery, leading to his breakthrough album, *The Incredible Jazz Guitar of Wes Montgomery*.

Montgomery suffered a fatal heart attack in 1968 when he was just 45 years old. Despite his brief career, he influenced guitarists across multiple genres, from jazz to rock and even fusion. His unique sound, effortless phrasing, and innovative approach continue to inspire musicians today.

JIM HALL (1930–2013)

Coming from a completely different school of talent, Jim Hall was a classically trained guitarist. Born in Buffalo, New York, in 1930, Hall started playing guitar at age 10. By the time he was a teenager, he'd already developed a passion for jazz, influenced by famous guitarist Charlie Christian and saxophonists such as Lester Young.

Hall's formal training set him apart from his contemporaries. He studied composition and classical guitar at the Cleveland Institute of Music, and this background in classical music profoundly shaped his style. Hall's playing emphasized subtlety, space, and harmonic sophistication, not speed or flash like many guitarists of the time. Hall was also known for his lyrical, understated approach, making every note count.

Beginning in the 1950s, Hall played with Chico Hamilton's quintet, where he honed his ability to blend seamlessly into ensembles rather than dominate them. Next, he joined the Jimmy Giuffre Trio, an experimental group of well-trained musicians that focused on blurring the lines between jazz and chamber music.

Hall's minimalist style demonstrated that guitar doesn't have to be loud or aggressive to be effective. Despite his quiet demeanor, Hall's impact on jazz guitar was immense. He helped shift the focus from rapid-fire solos to thoughtful, melodic storytelling. His career spanned over six decades, and even in his later years, he continued to push musical boundaries.

JAZZ OF THE 1970s AND 1980s

Jazz went through rapid-fire changes in the 1970s and he 1980s as the traditional styles of earlier decades gave way to bold experimentation and electric innovations. Jazz fusion emerged in the late 1960s, incorporating elements of rock, funk, and electronic music. The genre often features electric instruments and complex rhythms.

JOHN MCLAUGHLIN (b. 1942)

Born in Doncaster, England, in 1942, John McLaughlin grew up in a musical household. He first learned piano before transitioning to guitar at 11. Even at a young age, McLaughlin was drawn to blues and jazz and idolized Django Reinhardt and Charlie Christian. But unlike other guitarists of his time, McLaughlin wasn't solely influenced by traditional jazz. He found that Indian classical music, flamenco, and rock also spoke to him.

McLaughlin built his reputation as a session guitarist in London while working with various jazz and R&B artists. However, he became frustrated with the constraints of mainstream music and moved to New York City in 1969, where he quickly became part of the burgeoning jazz fusion movement.

When McLaughlin joined Miles Davis, his career took off. He played on groundbreaking albums such as *In a Silent Way* (1969) and *Bitches Brew* (1970), which experimented with electrified jazz. Davis was so impressed with McLaughlin's raw, aggressive style that he named a track on *Bitches Brew* after him.

In 1971, McLaughlin formed The Mahavishnu Orchestra, one of the most influential jazz fusion bands of all time. Their music marked a radical departure from traditional jazz, blending elements of progressive rock, Indian classical music, blues, and jazz improvisation into a completely new sound.

The band's compositions feature unusual time signatures, polyrhythms, and intricate harmonies. Their music was far more complex than standard rock or jazz, drawing comparisons to classical music in structure.

The name *Mahavishnu Orchestra* is deeply connected to John McLaughlin's spiritual beliefs. In the late 1960s, McLaughlin became a disciple of Indian spiritual guru Sri Chinmoy, who named him Mahavishnu, meaning "Great Vishnu," a Hindu deity associated with protection, preservation, and cosmic order.

By the mid-1970s, McLaughlin's obsession with Indian classical music led him to form Shakti, a groundbreaking acoustic group blending jazz with traditional Indian music. In direct contrast to McLaughlin's high-energy fusion days, Shakti featured intricate tabla rhythms, violin, and McLaughlin's use of the scalloped-fret acoustic guitar, which allowed him to mimic the fluidity of the Indian sitar.

Today, McLaughlin remains a living legend, proving that jazz guitar is limitless in its exploration of sound, culture, and technical expression.

AL DI MEOLA (b. 1954)

Al Di Meola, born in Jersey City, New Jersey, in 1954, is known for his blistering speed, precision, and Latin-jazz fusion. Di Meola loved mixing the intensity of rock with the complexity of jazz. He honed his skills at Berklee College of Music, and his big break came in 1974 when he was hired by Chick Corea to join Return to Forever, one of the most important fusion bands of the era.

Albums such as *Romantic Warrior* (1976) showcased Di Meola's virtuosic speed, complex rhythmic patterns, and mastery of alternate picking. Unlike traditional jazz guitarists, he embraced distortion and aggressive picking techniques, making his solos resemble rapid-fire machine gun bursts.

Di Meola's style evolved over the years as he explored softer, more melodic acoustic styles while still maintaining his signature intensity. His blending of Latin, classical, and jazz elements influenced countless guitarists, including fusion legends like Steve Morse and Guthrie Govan.

Still an active musician, Di Meola received an honorary doctorate of music from his alma mater, Berklee College of Music, in 2018. In 2023, he wrote a eulogy for Jeff Beck that spoke to the impact he had on Di Meola growing up.

JAZZ OF THE 1990s AND TODAY

In the 1990s, a revival of classical jazz took place while fusion and funk were still in the front row. Traditionalists honored bebop and swing, while others experimented with effects and rock influences.

Modern jazz guitarists seamlessly mix traditional jazz with rock, electronic, and world music. Streaming and digital platforms have also expanded the genre's reach globally. Jazz guitar is more diverse and boundary-pushing than ever, blending genres while keeping its roots alive.

BLUES MUSIC
AND THE GUITAR

BLUES MUSIC PRE-1900s

Blues has deep roots in African American spirituals, work songs, and field hollers from the Deep South, especially in Mississippi, Louisiana, and Alabama. These influences became central to blues, particularly the use of call-and-response vocal phrasing.

Most early blues musicians lacked formal instruments and had to use what was available, leading to the development of unique sounds and instruments. One such instrument was the diddley bow, a single-stringed slide instrument often built from broom wire and a wooden board. The banjo, which originated from African stringed instruments, was also widely used before the guitar became dominant.

As the genre developed, musicians began using homemade guitars, often crafted from cigar boxes, which allowed for the slide-playing technique that would later define Delta blues. One of the most significant musical developments in this era was the blues scale, which incorporated flattened third, fifth, and seventh notes to create the mournful, expressive sound that defines blues music. Even though this era of music was not recorded, it still left an impressive impact on the future of American music.

BLUES THROUGH THE 1920s

Over the next two decades, the birth of acoustic blues led to music with a much more structured form. During this period, the 12-bar blues progression became the standard framework, providing a repeatable chord structure that musicians could use to improvise melodies and lyrics.

One of the most significant developments of this era was the rise of Delta blues from the Mississippi Delta, which became known for its raw, emotional vocal delivery and innovative guitar techniques. Characterized by solo performances, slide guitar, and harmonica, Delta blues often explored themes of hardship and the African American experience.

Around the same time, Texas blues was also evolving but with a more lyrical style and rhythmic sound. Texas blues often used a smoother, melodic structure that focused on intricate picking patterns and storytelling.

Blues music spread quickly because of traveling musicians, also called "songsters," who performed in all venues. As songsters journeyed across the South, they brought regional variations of blues with them.

DJANGO REINHARDT (1910–1953)

Reinhardt, a Romani-French guitarist, transformed guitar music with his unique phrasing, expressive vibrato, and intricate single-note lines, all of which would influence blues guitarists for generations.

Reinhardt was born on January 23, 1910, in Liberchies, Belgium, into a family of traveling musicians. He fell in love with music at an early age. Growing up in encampments around Paris, he first learned violin and banjo before transitioning to the guitar. By the time he was a teenager, he was a prodigy, playing professionally and blending traditional Romani music with musette (French dance music) and early blues-inspired American recordings.

Despite his early success, Reinhardt's life took a tragic turn in 1928 when his caravan caught fire, leaving him with severe burns. The damage to his left hand was so extreme that he lost the use of two fingers. Doctors told him he would never play guitar again, but Reinhardt refused to quit. He developed a completely new technique, using only his index and middle fingers for solos while incorporating sweeping arpeggios and fast single-note runs to compensate for his injury. This adaptation would later influence blues guitarists like B.B. King and Eric Clapton, who admired Reinhardt's ability to convey deep emotion through fewer notes.

Reinhardt's exposure to American blues and jazz recordings in the 1930s influenced his playing, and his use of slides, bending, and vibrato became hallmarks of blues guitar. His ability to improvise fluid, soulful melodies over simple chord progressions was a precursor to the call-and-response phrasing found in blues solos.

During World War II, Reinhardt remained in occupied France, a dangerous place for a Romani musician, as the Nazis actively persecuted his people. Despite the risks, he continued to perform and even attempted to escape to Switzerland at one point. After the war, his influence spread to the U.S., leading to a tour with Duke Ellington. Although he struggled with the growing dominance of electric guitars, his acoustic style remained timeless.

In the early 1950s, Reinhardt withdrew from public life, preferring to fish and spend time with his family. He made a brief return to recording, showcasing an evolved, more blues-influenced tone, before passing away from a stroke in 1953 at just 43 years old.

ROBERT JOHNSON (1911–1938)

Johnson is known as one of the most mysterious figures in music history. Born into poverty in Hazlehurst, Mississippi, Johnson was initially an unremarkable guitarist who struggled to make a name for himself. Accounts that Johnson disappeared for months and came back as one of the most talented musicians in the world have given rise to one of the most famous legends in music history.

The legend goes that Johnson met the Devil at a crossroads at midnight and sold his soul for unparalleled guitar mastery. While an interesting story, the reality is that Johnson left to train obsessively, learning from masters like Son House and Willie Brown.

Johnson's influential fingerpicking techniques gave the illusion of two guitars being played at once. During his career, he only recorded 29 songs, including "Cross Road Blues" and "Sweet Home Chicago."

While his legacy lived on in future musicians like Eric Clapton, Keith Richards, and Bob Dylan, Johnson's life was tragically short at just 27 years. It's commonly believed that he was poisoned, but no formal autopsy was ever performed. Rumors abound, including that a jealous husband killed Johnson after discovering his wife's affair or that the Devil came for his soul. Regardless of the cause of his death, Johnson was an amazing guitarist.

BLUES OF THE 1930s AND 1940s

A real change occurred in blues music with the introduction of the electric guitar in 1932 and the Great Migration that took place between 1910 and 1970. Millions of Black Americans moved out of the rural South to urban areas like Chicago, Detroit, and Memphis, bringing their blues traditions with them. Small juke joints were replaced with larger venues to accommodate growing demand. Bigger audiences, in turn, meant that amplified instruments were needed to be heard over the noise of the crowd.

The electric guitar's addition to blues music is credited to T-Bone Walker, but other changes were happening in cities like Chicago. Musicians such as Big Bill Broonzy began switching from acoustic to electric guitars, and blues bands added bass, drums, piano, and harmonica to create a richer, more powerful sound. Blues music became louder, grittier, and more rhythmic, forming the foundation of what would soon be known as Chicago blues.

The advent of recorded music accelerated the spread of all genres, leading to the rise of national stars that record labels could advertise, promoting the music even farther.

T-BONE WALKER (1910–1975)

Born Aaron Thibeaux Walker in Linden, Texas, Walker grew up in a musical family in Dallas and was performing professionally by his teens. As a teenager, Walker was protégé to Blind Lemon

Jefferson, giving him the chance to learn from Jefferson while acting as his guide.

In the early 1940s, Walker made history playing blues on an electric guitar for the first time. His breakthrough hit, "Call It Stormy Monday (But Tuesday Is Just as Bad)," was melodic, expressive, and technically advanced. It became a huge success.

Not only was his sound revolutionary, but Walker's showmanship also set him apart. He played the guitar behind his head, with his teeth, or while doing the splits, influencing future performers like Chuck Berry, Jimi Hendrix, and Stevie Ray Vaughan. He was inducted into both the Blues Hall of Fame and the Rock and Roll Hall of Fame, and his 1969 album *Good Feelin'* won a Grammy Award for Best Ethnic or Traditional Folk Recording.

BIG BILL BROONZY (ca. 1893–1958)

Born Lee Conley Bradley in either Mississippi or Arkansas—the details of his birth are highly debated—Big Bill Broonzy rose from humble beginnings to become an American blues star. After World War I, he moved to Chicago, where he captivated audiences with his country and folk-influenced acoustic blues style.

Broonzy was comfortable in both solo acoustic settings and full-band arrangements. His ability to blend traditional folk-blues with the rising urban electric sound made him a bridge between eras. His style incorporated his booming voice, fingerpicking, and narrative songwriting.

Not only did Broonzy achieve fame in the U.S., but he also toured Europe and took the American blues sound international. He achieved recognition as a top-selling blues recording artist by 1940 and toured Europe in 1951. He was inducted into the Blues Foundation Hall of Fame in 1980. Broonzy's career helped establish blues as a respected genre and set the stage for the global blues revival of the 1960s.

BLUES OF THE 1950s

The 1950s were the golden age of blues music. This was especially true in Chicago, where the genre was thriving, and Chicago blues would lay the foundation for modern rock and roll.

At the center of it all was the electric guitar, which went from a supporting rhythm instrument to the lead voice of the band. Amplification allowed guitarists to cut through the noise of busy clubs and helped shape a raw, emotionally charged style.

MUDDY WATERS (ca. 1913–1983)

Born McKinley Morganfield in Issaquena County, Mississippi, Muddy Waters grew up on the Stovall Plantation near Clarksdale, where he was exposed to the Delta blues tradition. He learned to play the harmonica and acoustic guitar, which—along with his deep, powerful voice—set him apart and soon gained him performances locally.

In 1943, Waters moved to Chicago in search of new opportunities. There, he found his acoustic style drowned out by the noise of crowded clubs, but he adapted quickly and took up the electric guitar. With songs like "Rollin' Stone," "Hoochie Coochie Man," and "Got My Mojo Working," Muddy Waters helped define the Chicago blues sound.

However, Waters's influence stretched far beyond Chicago and directly influenced the British blues explosion of the 1960s. Artists like the Rolling Stones (who named themselves after his song), Eric Clapton, and Led Zeppelin drew heavily from his sound.

Waters was dubbed "The Father of Modern Chicago Blues" and received six Grammy Awards for Best Ethnic or Traditional Folk Recording. In 1987, he was inducted posthumously into the Rock and Roll Hall of Fame, and he received the Grammy Lifetime Achievement Award in 1992.

BLUES OF THE 1960s AND THE RISE OF ROCK

In the 1960s, the blues underwent a transformation. Love for electric blues guitar was rapidly growing overseas. Rabid interest, particularly in Britain, helped launch the genre into the global spotlight.

In the U.S., blues was losing its mainstream popularity, but in the UK, young guitarists like Eric Clapton, Jimmy Page, and Keith Richards were discovering American blues records and using them as the foundation for what would become the British blues explosion.

JIMI HENDRIX (1942–1970)

Born in Seattle, Washington, Jimi Hendrix grew up in poverty to alcoholic parents. Hendrix's father had difficulty a job, and his parents divorced when he was nine. Hendrix and his siblings were in and out of foster care, occasionally living with various relatives.

Faced with neglect and instability, Hendrix struggled to find something to hold onto in his tumultuous life. He found a one-stringed ukelele in the garbage and, note by note, began to pick out Elvis Presley songs by ear. Music became his refuge, and he taught himself to play on a five-dollar acoustic guitar.

Despite—or maybe because of—his lack of formal training, Hendrix developed an innovative style that was uniquely his own. He combined the deep soul of the blues with the raw power of rock and layered it all with psychedelic flair. He moved to London in 1966, where he gained attention from the world with his band, the Jimi Hendrix Experience.

Amazing crowds with hits like "Purple Haze," "Hey Joe," and "Voodoo Child," Hendrix performed flashy onstage antics—playing guitar behind his back, with his teeth, or even setting it on fire. While he put on a good performance, his true genius was his sound. He mastered the use of distortion, feedback, and effects pedals, creating musical textures no one had heard before.

Hendrix shattered common perception of what electric guitars could accomplish, inspiring generations of guitarists across all genres. However, like many of his contemporaries, Hendrix struggle with substance abuse and passed away at the young age of 27 from barbiturate-related asphyxia.

Despite his short career, the Rock and Roll Hall of Fame described him as "arguably the greatest instrumentalist in the history of rock music." He was inducted into its ranks as part of the Jimi Hendrix Experience in 1992.

ERIC CLAPTON (b. 1945)

A native of Surrey, England, Eric Clapton was deeply inspired by American blues and focused on infusing blues authenticity with rock energy. Classic songs such as "Layla," "Tears in Heaven," and "Crossroads" combine the genres into amazing and unique pieces.

"Layla," one of his most famous songs, tells a story of unrequited love. "Tears in Heaven" is a heart-wrenching lament for his son, who fell to his death at just four years old. "Crossroads" goes in another direction entirely, bringing high energy to a blues-rock anthem to showcase yet another side of Clapton's talent.

As of March 2025, Eric Clapton remains an active figure in the music world but has slowed down since his retirement in 2015. He's the only artist to be inducted into the Rock and Roll Hall of Fame three times and has received 18 Grammy Awards. He still does limited tours and releases new music, continuing to influence the music world.

BLUES AND ROCK
OF THE 1970s

The 1970s became a defining era for blues and rock as musicians pushed the boundaries of the genres to create new sounds. While blues remained rooted in expressive bends and emotional storytelling, the decade saw a shift toward heavier, electrified tones. Rock guitar became louder, faster, and more aggressive, driven by advancements in amplification and effects.

The rise of arena rock meant that guitarists played to larger audiences, leading to theatrical, high-energy performances. The explosive popularity of rock music with guitar-driven sounds dominated charts and stadiums worldwide. As rock evolved, the blues — while still influential — began to take a backseat.

As the 1980s arrived, rock expanded even further, giving rise to glam metal and shred guitar. Blues continued to influence some rock subgenres, but the overall sound leaned more toward polished production, flashy performances, and commercial appeal. MTV also played a crucial role in shaping the next era of rock, making images and visual spectacles just as important as the music itself.

JIMMY PAGE (b. 1944)

Born in a London suburb, Page found his first instrument, a mysteriously abandoned Spanish guitar, in his home as a child. Although he took a few lessons, he was primarily self-taught and influenced by rockabilly guitarists. His career began in the London session scene, where he became a widely sought-after session guitarist.

Page formed Led Zeppelin in 1968, and the band cemented his place as a music legend. Page created some of the most recognizable riffs in rock history. His use of the violin bow on electric guitar and dramatic stage presence made him a rock icon.

Jimmy Page was inducted into the Rock and Roll Hall of Fame twice, first with The Yardbirds in 1992, then with Led Zeppelin in 1995. He won a Grammy Lifetime Achievement Award in 2005 for his contributions to music with Led Zeppelin and received Kennedy Center Honors in 2012. In addition, *Rolling Stone* ranked Page as number three on their list of the "100 Greatest Guitarists of All Time," cementing his legacy as one of rock's most influential musicians.

BLUES AND ROCK OF THE 1980s AND 1990s

In the 1980s, rock became increasingly commercially driven, while blues remained largely out of the mainstream. Glam metal was extremely popular, but going into the 1990s, rock moved away from the polished sound of the 1980s as grunge and alternative rock gained popularity. These subgenres stripped rock down with simpler yet heavier riffs and raw lyrics. The over-the-top guitar solos of the 1980s faded, replaced by a focus on tone, mood, and songwriting.

EDDIE VAN HALEN (1955–2020)

Born in the Netherlands, Eddie Van Halen started with classical piano but later switched to guitar. He developed his skills by playing along with records from his favorite groups. In the early 1970s, he and his brother, Alex, formed Van Halen.

Eddie's signature two-handed tapping, showcased in "Eruption," popularized the technique, which allows guitarists to execute fast, fluid runs across the fretboard. His use of whammy bar dives, harmonics, and custom modifications to guitars and amps led to new possibilities in rock music.

However, the "brown sound," a warm yet powerful distortion, became Van Halen's sonic trademark. Van Halen helped define the sound of 1980s rock, blending technical mastery with infectious songwriting.

STEVIE RAY VAUGHAN (1954–1990)

Born and raised in Dallas, Texas, Vaughan's childhood was filled with music. Inspired by his brother, Jimmie, to pick up the guitar at a very young age, he dropped out of school at 18. After moving to Austin, he gained a following playing gigs in local clubs, refining his fiery, soulful style.

In 1978, Vaughan formed Double Trouble, a powerhouse blues-rock trio that gained national attention. Vaughan's aggressive picking, deep vibrato, and signature tone set him apart as a modern blues icon.

Throughout the 1980s, he reignited interest in blues, inspiring a new wave of guitarists. Tragically, his life was cut short in a helicopter crash in 1990, but his sudden death couldn't erase the profound impact he had on all genres of music, particularly the new life he breathed into the blues.

BLUES AND ROCK OF THE 2000s

Since the turn of the century, blues and rock guitar have evolved, blending classic influences with modern innovation. While neither genre dominates mainstream charts like they once did, both remain alive through dedicated artists and a thriving underground scene.

Blues has resurfaced in the work of musicians like Joe Bonamassa, Gary Clark Jr., and Keb' Mo', who blend traditional blues with rock, soul, and R&B. These artists fuse genres to create unique sounds with powerful vocals and a storytelling, pushing blues past its traditional structure while still maintaining its soul.

Rock has diversified into many subgenres like indie and alternative. Guitar-driven rock remains central in groups like The White Stripes, Arctic Monkeys, Foo Fighters, and The Black Keys, whose stripped-down, gritty sound echoes garage and blues-rock traditions. Meanwhile, John Mayer brought bluesy guitar solos into pop-rock, earning respect from both casual listeners and serious players.

While blues and rock guitar may not be mainstream's loudest voices today, their influence is everywhere. From classic-style riffs to genre-blending innovation, modern guitarists continue to honor tradition while crafting something entirely new.

TOP MODERN ROCK AND BLUES ARTISTS AND HITS

JOE BONAMASSA (b. 1977)

A modern blues virtuoso skilled at combining technical mastery and soulful phrasing, Bonamassa brings traditional blues to audiences of all ages. His top hit is "Driving Towards the Daylight."

GARY CLARK JR. (b. 1984)

Clark is a pro at fusing blues, rock, soul, and hip-hop with fiery guitar solos. He brings an electrifying presence to every performance, especially his hit "Bright Lights."

THE WHITE STRIPES

Jack White's raw, minimalist guitar tone revived garage rock in the early twenty-first century. The riff from "Seven Nation Army" has become one of the most recognizable in modern music, proving that you don't need complexity to be iconic.

THE BLACK KEYS

This rock duo's stripped-down sound is showcased in songs like their hit "Lonely Boy." Dan Auerbach's riff-driven style blends vintage tone with modern edge and has revived gritty guitar music for the mainstream.

CONCLUSION

Having learned about the history, anatomy, styles, techniques, and cultural impact of one of the most amazing and beloved instruments in the world, you're now ready to take your next steps as a guitarist.

From humble beginnings to its legendary status in many genres, the guitar has proven itself to be more than just an instrument; the guitar is a cultural voice and creative outlet. It could also be a lifelong companion for you.

No matter where you are on your musical journey, there's always more to learn, more to discover, and more to share. Take a moment to reflect on how far you've come since you first thought about the guitar as your instrument of choice.

As you master the guitar, the time will come to take it out from behind closed doors and share your music with others. Performance is where practice meets purpose. It gives you the chance to demonstrate your technical ability and the creativity of your emotions.

Don't let nerves or self-doubt be a reason for failure. Prepare thoroughly and remember that confidence comes from experience. Practice not just your music but also your transitions, posture, facial expressions, and even breathing. Perform for small groups of family and friends or even just in front of a mirror. Knowing the material gives you the foundation to trust yourself.

Not every performance needs to be at a large venue — get your feet wet by playing in low-pressure environments at first to ease into the experience and build confidence step by step. Look for local opportunities like open mic nights.

All musicians make mistakes, so when you're performing, don't focus on small imperfections. Most of the time, the audience won't even notice if you make a mistake. Just keep playing. Shift your mindset away from perfectionism and toward expression. If your music moves someone emotionally, that matters more than impeccable technique.

While you're playing, make sure to connect with your audience by making eye contact, smiling, and letting them feel your passion for the music. When you're genuinely enjoying yourself, it shows — and it's contagious. All great musicians possess passion for their music, and that's why they're remembered.

Guitars will continue to evolve, and while you've explored their rich history, you may wonder what the future holds. Technology is expanding possibilities, from loop pedals and amp modeling to smart guitars with built-in tuners.

Today, guitarists can blend analog tone with digital precision. Artists like Tash Sultana, Ed Sheeran, and Tom Misch have pioneered new sounds by combining live playing with looping stations and digital layers. Future guitarists may never be limited by the boundaries of genre or gear.

Artificial intelligence will also play a role in changing the way guitars are played and music is created. Apps, interactive tabs, and AI-based tools are making it easier than ever to learn guitar. Platforms like Yousician, Fender Play, and JustinGuitar allow players of all levels to improve through real-time feedback and structured lessons. In the future, AI may even be able to adapt to your playing style, offer personalized practice routines, and even jam with you.

Artists no longer need to rely on record labels to make music. You can record, mix, and release music entirely from your home. Online platforms like Bandcamp, SoundCloud, YouTube, and TikTok allow you to share your music globally within seconds. Who knows? The next guitar legend could be recording in their bedroom right now.

More and more, we're seeing the guitar cross cultural and musical boundaries. It's as likely to appear in hip-hop, electronic music, and indie folk as in blues or metal. In the coming years, expect to see even more global collaboration and hybrid styles, blending traditional techniques with new rhythms, lyrical approaches, and storytelling traditions.

The guitar isn't fading away — it's just entering its next great era. This instrument is more than six strings and a piece of wood; it's a portal to creativity, emotion, community, and self-discovery. The guitar has been shaped by centuries of players — and now, it's your turn to sculpt its future.

Whether you dream of playing to crowds of thousands or you simply want to master your favorite songs, this musical journey is uniquely yours. Wherever it takes you, be proud of how far you've come. Keep your fingers moving, your heart open, and your ears curious.

Perform with passion. Practice with purpose. Play with joy.

And most importantly… never stop playing.

www.ingramcontent.com/pod-product-compliance
Lightning Source LLC
Chambersburg PA
CBHW071753120626
46550CB00002B/773